Using Your
Chakras

Also by Ruth White

The River of Life
Working with Your Chakras
Working with Your Guides and Angels

Using Your Chakras

A New Approach to Healing Your Life

Ruth White

BARNES & NOBLE

NEW YORK

Contents

Acknowledgements

I should like to thank the groups I teach for their support and for asking the right questions at the right time, so that the work continues to unfold.

Names and identifying details in the case studies have been changed but I should like to thank all who gave such generous permission for their life experiences to be used in this way.

Once again I wish to mention my Jack Russell dog, Jackson, who has been a warm, constant and patient companion at workshops and beside me at my word-processor throughout the writing process.

Introduction

This book builds on the foundations laid in its predecessor, *Working With Your Chakras*. Though each book is complete in itself, it is recommended that you use them together to get the deepest understanding of the chakra system and how working with it can help your life and spiritual development.

Working With Your Chakras set out basic information about chakras and explained how to recognize chakra energies, to explore, heal and enhance the function of the chakras themselves. It gave information about chakra colours, fragrances and crystals, with suggestions as to how to use these in chakra work.

For easy reference, this book also has pages setting out the basic information required for working with each chakra but it moves on from the work on chakra sensitivity to look at ways in which deeper chakra knowledge can enable you to reach your full physical, emotional, mental and spiritual potential and give you the tools with which to improve or heal every life situation.

Working With Your Chakras explored each chakra systematically, from the root to the crown, whereas this book is arranged in chapters relating to different aspects of life. In this way, if you need help, with family relationships for instance, you can turn directly to Chapter 4 to find those chakras with which to work in order to build strengths or to bring healing.

Firstly, though, let us remind ourselves of how this particular system of chakra work has evolved and set the scene for the use of this book.

Chapter 1

About Chakras and Chakra Work

Gildas, my discarnate guide and communicator, has been in direct teaching communication with me for almost forty years, but I have been aware of his presence beside me since early childhood. He tells me that his last incarnation on earth was as a Benedictine monk in fourteenth-century France. He is now working with a large group of guides from 'the other side' in order to establish clearer connections between the dimensions and to give spiritual help and teaching to those of us who are in incarnation.

When I attune to his vibration, I hear his words and teachings like a kind of dictation which I can repeat onto tape or write down. As part of his communication, Gildas gives teaching about healing. He talks of the channelling of subtle energies through one person to another, in order to aid healing and growth. Awareness of the energy system long recognized in Eastern esoteric teaching as the Chakras is a tool which helps in working with healing growth. Gildas has adapted the original Eastern chakra knowledge to make it more understandable and applicable within the Western tradition and it is this system that I share in this book. Gildas encourages us to see the chakras as a Map of Consciousness, which enables us to discover more about our individual and collective purpose. Furthermore, it enables us to use chakra work to heal our lives and fulfil true potential.

Awakening to your chakras heightens and intensifies your spiritual awareness but, important as this is, spirituality cannot truly flourish unless you are also on a pathway to fulfilment and growth in life as a whole. Your spirituality cannot find true expression unless you are a whole being – healthy in mind, body, emotion *and* spirit.

Through chakra work you can improve your relationships with family, friends, lovers, partners, colleagues and bosses; release blockages around such issues as sex, money and authority; understand more about your sense of purpose in order to find greater satisfaction in your work and more certainty about the direction you want to take in life; nurture the courage to make major life changes; enhance your confidence and psychological stature and discover subtle tools with which to heal yourself and others so bringing you greater physical health and vitality.

ORIGINAL TEACHINGS

Original teachings about the subtle energy system known as 'the chakras' come from Eastern esoteric writings in which the language used is Sanskrit. The Sanskrit word *chakrum* means 'wheel'. Properly speaking, *chakrum* is the singular form and *chakra* the plural but in the West it is usual to speak of one *chakra* and many *chakras*. I follow this Western practice throughout my books and teaching work. When seen clairvoyantly, chakras are wondrous wheels of light and colour: shimmering, turning and vibrating, feeding and reflecting our subtle life energies.

Sanskrit descriptions customarily refer to seven chakras as forming the major system, with some teachers acknowledging an extra, eighth chakra. More recently much channelled information, including that from Gildas, has spoken of additional major chakras which are in a process of awakening. These extra chakras usually expand the major system to twelve.

THE AURA

Around every human being there is an energy field known as the aura. This may be clairvoyantly perceived in full colour or as a vague light. It usually stretches 4 to 6 inches or 10 to 15 centimetres out from the physical body. Though some of our basic aura colours never change, others vary according to our mood or state of health at any given moment and can be indicators of these. Once a person is truly dead there is no longer an aura or energy field. A vital essence is withdrawn.

Much of the colour and energy of the auric field is supplied by the chakras, which are wheels of light and colour interpenetrating with (affecting and affected by) the physical body. Chakras also carry links to specific parts of the physical glandular system and might therefore be described as subtle glands.

CHAKRA COLOURS

Each chakra is associated with a particular colour in the spectrum and needs to produce this colour for its energy field. The root chakra produces red; the sacral, orange; the solar plexus, yellow; the heart, green; the throat, blue; the brow, indigo; the crown, violet. The alter major produces brown. Healthy chakra colours are bright but transparent, like those produced by a rainbow or those seen when sunlight passes through stained glass.

In healing and chakra work, the primary colour notes may have to be modified. It will also be seen that more than one colour is important to each chakra, that any colour may healthily be present in any chakra and even that each chakra produces its own spectrum. Difficulties arise when a chakra is not producing enough of its 'home colour' for complete health and well-being. Much chakra healing work is dependent on the use and visualization of colour and there is full reference to the significant colours and their meanings in each section.

NAMES AND LOCATIONS OF THE CHAKRAS

On page 7 the diagram shows the seven major chakras, plus one extra (the Alter Major), and their positions in relation to the physical body. They are named in descending order as Crown, Brow, Alter Major, Throat, Heart, Solar Plexus, Sacral and Root. Semantic difficulties can arise simply because there is a variety of terminology, some of which is Eastern and some more Westernized. For instance, different teachers use the terms 'Sacral', 'Hara' or 'Spleen', to refer to the chakra which is two fingers below the navel. Confusion of terminology around 'Brow', 'Ajna' or 'Third Eye' also sometimes occurs. Problems arise if these terms are used interchangeably within the usual sevenfold system, when minor or additional chakras come under discussion, and when those newly awakening chakras which are now becoming a part of the major system are named. In Chapter 12 the new chakras are described and some terms which have previously been used interchangeably are used more specifically.

Most Eastern traditions describe a sevenfold major chakra system, while acknowledging varying large numbers of minor chakras throughout the body. Students of the famous medium and esotericist Alice Bailey (see Bibliography), will know that she spoke of an eighth chakra, giving it the Latin name 'Alta Major'. This chakra is included as an important one here, but with the spelling 'Alter Major', meaning 'other' rather than 'higher' major.

The expanded major chakra system suggests a total of twelve major points to which we should direct attention in order to

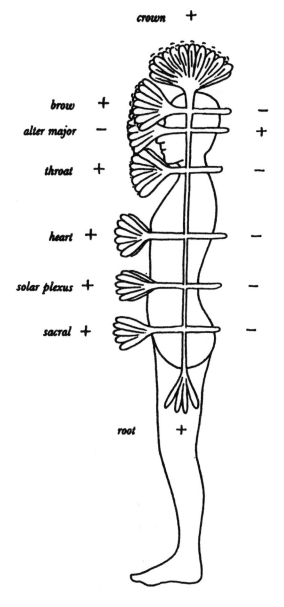

crown +

brow +

alter major −

throat +

heart +

solar plexus +

sacral +

root +

−

+

−

−

−

−

The seven best-known chakras, plus the alter major. Energy flows from positive to negative (+ = positive polarity, − = negative polarity) and up and down the central column. Note the reversed polarity of the alter major.

aid self-healing and growth. The number twelve is certainly important in other ways. We have twelve astrological signs, twelve calendar months in a year, and it is expected that twelve planets will eventually be discovered.

It is sometimes assumed that the words 'higher' or 'lower', in relation to Chakras, are used as terms of evaluation. But it is important to remember that these words are mainly descriptive of the chakra positions in the physical body when upright. There is no hierarchical system within the chakras – each one is a part of a team.

There is sometimes a lack of agreement as to whether the chakras are situated at the front or back of the body and its auric field. The diagram on page 7 attempts to depict the way in which chakras interpenetrate with the physical body, having 'petals' at the front and 'stems' at the back which project into the auric field.

CHAKRA PETALS, STEMS AND POLARITIES

There is a central subtle column of energy interpenetrating with the physical body and running from the crown of the head to the perineum (the area midway between the anus and the genitals). Each chakra has petals and a stem, except some of the new ones (see Chapter 12). The stems of the crown and the root chakras are open but contained within the central column. The other chakras have petals which open into the auric field at the front and stems which project into the auric field at the back. The stems normally stay closed but the petals are flexible, opening and closing, vibrating and turning, according to the different life situations encountered. A healthy chakra is a flexible chakra. Where there is dis-ease the chakra energies become inflexible or actually blocked, affecting our physical, mental, emotional and spiritual health.

Though normally closed, a healthy chakra stem is like a self-opening valve. It allows unwanted energy or reaction to pass through. It is part of the elimination system. Chakra stems can be damaged by shock or trauma, by over-use of drugs (medical or hallucinogenic), by lengthy or too frequent anaesthesia, and by abuse of alcohol or tobacco. In such cases they may stay open, rendering the individual vulnerable to outside influences of all kinds. This open state of the stems can be healed through an understanding of colour and energies, and by receiving the sort of healing which can be channelled through the hands. Much chakra work, though, is of a self-help nature. With a little knowledge you can do a great deal to change your life, with exercises which are almost as straighforward as breathing or through creative and colourful visualizations.

With the exception of the alter major chakra (see page 224), the petals carry a positive, and the stems a negative, polarity (see diagram on page 7). Again, these terms are not evaluatory but are rather used in an electrical or magnetic sense.

THE CHAKRA AREAS OF INFLUENCE

At the beginning of each chapter you will find a list of areas of influence. Besides the location and colours of the chakra under discussion, the list includes the following references:

Key Words
These words summarize the main aspects of life, feeling or spiritual development with which the chakra is connected.

Developmental Age
The first five chakras have a developmental age. This does not mean that a new-born baby only has a root chakra (developmental age 0–3/5 years), since every living person must have all the chakras for full spectrum functioning. Rather, it means that at certain ages particular chakras develop more strongly and their areas of influence are particularly operative. If childhood needs are met well enough at each developmental

age then the chakras will strengthen and develop normally. Where there are difficulties at the developmental ages the chakras may be adversely affected. When, later on, you realize that something in your life is out of balance, healing the appropriate chakra will help heal the original trauma or imbalance as well as the existential discomposure (see also the inner child, page 91).

Element

Each chakra has its own element. Its areas of influence are affected by that element and related to it. Life issues connected with earth, for instance, will usually belong to the root chakra. Germane issues may also be connected to the element of the chakra through a more symbolic interpretation of the element. Thus, earth (root) is connected with the sense of smell, as well as matter, nurturing, rooting, basic physiological needs and the physical body. Likewise, water (sacral) is connected to the sense of taste, the emotions, the flow of life, flexibility, sexuality, creativity, power, empowerment; and the water and blood within the physical body. Fire (solar plexus) is connected to the sense of sight, individuality, identity, vision, symbolic digestion of life and the physical digestive system. Air (heart) is connected to the sense of touch, as well as tenderness, detachment, the symbolic breath of life and to breathing and circulation in the physical body.

Akasha, a rather esoteric element (throat), is linked to the sound and colour in the universe and is the layer around us on which personal and collective memory is engraved; it is connected with the sense of hearing and also with expression, communication, the ability to listen, making ourselves heard and responsibility. Radium (brow) is connected to higher vibrations, spiritual vision, refinement and inspiration. Finally, magnetum (crown) is an element given for this chakra by several guides. It is not yet included in any comprehensive list of the elements we know, as it is still to be scientifically discovered. It is connected to the pull between gravity and levity and the process of incarnation.

Sense

Each of the first five chakras is associated with a sense, which also connects with the element, as we have seen. The root is linked to smell; the sacral to taste; the solar plexus to sight; the heart to touch; the throat to hearing.

Body

We have already spoken of the aura and the subtle layers which it represents. Each layer of the aura and each chakra is connected to a subtle body or plane. The relationships between these bodies and layers can be immensely complex. At the risk of over-simplifying, here is a brief summary:

- **The root and the red areas of the aura** are linked to the physical body.
- **The sacral and the orange areas of the aura** are linked to the etheric body. This body, being closest in vibration to the physical, holds a subtle replica or etheric double of every organ in the body and of the body itself. The etheric aspect of an organ does not withdraw from the body when the physical organ is removed. The etheric body only totally withdraws when death occurs.
- **The solar plexus and the yellow areas of the aura** are linked to the astral body and plane. Our astral bodies are refined and fluid in texture. People who have near-death experiences move into their astral body. Sometimes anaesthesia, abuse, a shock, accident, or dream state will induce the experience of being able to hover above the physical body, seeing everything which is happening to it, but not feeling its pain or sensations. The astral body is connected to the physical by a subtle energy cord. At death this cord is finally severed and the animated spirit or being of the person is no longer able to return to the current physical body but moves

on to the astral plane to be welcomed and aided through the initial experiences of death. The higher astral planes hold many healing temples. The lower astral planes (particularly at the interface between the etheric and astral layers) hold thought forms, many of which are negative.

- **The heart and the green areas of the aura** are linked to the feeling body. This is not to be confused with the emotional layer of our beings. Used in this sense, feeling means the ability to feel without being dominated by emotion and to empathize to the degree where we actually feel that we know how another person functions and what it is like to be them. This state may be experienced during sexual intercourse. It is also met when contemplating and empathizing with trees, plants, animals or crystals. We enter the feeling body when we are in true meditation, sometimes in dreams, when we communicate with guides and angels, or experience altered states of consciousness. Guides and angels use the feeling planes as an interface to which they come in order to meet us.

- **The throat and the blue areas of the aura** are linked to the lower mental body or plane. These are the areas where we experience the ability to name something. Once it is named it becomes a part of our world and comprehension. Before it is named it is too abstract for us to experience in the full consciousness of the finite mind. The receiving of symbols is one of the steps towards the naming process. The lower mental body is the vehicle through which truths and insights come from the personal unconscious, the collective unconscious and from the workings of the universe itself.

- **The brow and the indigo areas of the aura** are linked to the spirit and the higher mental body, the stage beyond the lower mental body or plane where there are energies and forces which are beyond our finite comprehension. Part of the angelic stream of consciousness exists on this level, as does the pure energy of divine principles. Angels and guides help us make the transition between the higher and lower mental planes to the finite mind.

- **The crown and the violet areas of the aura** are linked to the soul and the causal body. The soul carries the record of our evolution, knows the causes we have set in motion, and the effects we must balance, redeem and transcend. It is at this level that we make many choices which affect the conditions of our lives on earth. (see Chapter 2, page 24, and entry for 'karma' in the Glossary).

The Glandular Connection

Each chakra is related to a gland or several glands in the physical body. The chakras can therefore be seen as a subtle addition to the glandular system. Healing the relevant chakras will help glandular function.

In the system used by Gildas, the root chakra is connected to the gonads (ovaries in women and testes in men); the sacral is connected to the lymph system; the solar plexus to the adrenals; the heart to the thymus; the throat to the thyroid; the brow to the pineal; and the crown to the pituitary.

Quietening and Stimulating Fragrances

There are fragrances recommended for balancing each of the chakras. They are best bought in concentrated oil form, as used in aromatherapy. If mixed with a carrier oil, such as sweet almond or jojoba, they can be used directly on the body, for massage, or in the bath. Undiluted, a few drops can be added to water in a fragrance burner to perfume a room. Many of them can also be obtained in the form of joss sticks or incense cones. Suggestions for their use according to the specific concerns of this book are given in the exercise section of each chapter.

Crystals and Gemstones

There are specific crystals which relate to each chakra (see the Glossary, and the exercise section of each chapter, for suggestions about working with crystals).

Affirmations and Prayers

Affirmations are phrases which we reiterate mentally when we wish to change our behaviour or belief systems. Prayers are an appeal to a higher authority to help us to new realizations or to aid us in changing our lives. The words given for each chakra can be used as affirmations and/or prayers.

CHAKRA PAIRS

The important connections between particular pairs and groups of chakras are explored in depth, together with the areas of life affected by their interactions.

Firstly, each chakra needs to be considered as a pair with those which come before and after it in the energy system. Thus, in the sevenfold system, root pairs with sacral, sacral with solar plexus, solar plexus with heart, heart with throat, throat with brow, and brow with crown. With the inclusion of the alter major, throat and alter major become a pair, as do alter major and brow.

Other chakra pairings are linked with their colours. Each colour of the spectrum has its scientific complement. For example, if you look intently at something which is bright red and then close your eyes or look towards a blank wall, the 'after image' will be green, and vice versa. Thus red and green are known as complementary colours. The root chakra colour is red and the heart chakra is green, so the root and heart form an important pair in the chakra team. In the same way, orange and blue are complementary colours and the pairing between the sacral chakra and the throat is very strong indeed.

Yellow and purple complement each other, so the yellow solar plexus pairs with both the purple chakras – the brow and the crown.

The vital energy flow between root/crown and crown/root (see page 21) makes these two centres another key pair.

The crown chakra is the seat of the higher will, whilst the heart is the seat of incarnate wisdom. Much of our evolution depends on establishing a link between these.

The solar plexus is the seat of the lower will. Success in fulfilling our highest purpose is enhanced when higher and lower wills work smoothly together, hence crown and solar plexus form an interconnective pair.

The root and the alter major are both linked to our instincts, sense of self-preservation and early warning systems, and so form a pair that is essential in enhancing our connection with earth and the natural world.

With notable connections between root and heart, root and crown and crown and heart, these three also form a chakra group. Other groups include the solar plexus, brow and crown; the first five chakras (root, sacral, solar plexus, heart and throat); and the three main head chakras (throat, brow and crown).

Each of these pairs and groupings reflects a particular area of our lives.

ARCHETYPES

By dictionary definition these are 'primordial images inherited by all'. Each human society is affected by forces such as peace, war, beauty, justice, wisdom, healing, death, birth, love, power. The essence of these defies definition and we need images, myths, symbols and personifications to help us in understanding the depth and breadth of them. Tarot cards, which have ancient origins, have twenty-two personified or symbolized archetypes in the major arcana. These cover most aspects of human experience.

We can come to a deeper understanding of the chakras if we study those archetypes which are most directly or deeply connected with them. In considering pairs and groups of chakras, working with certain archetypes can serve to clarify the chakra relationships and to give us a fuller comprehension of our life aims, drives and blockages. Archetypes can be great healers when we know enough about them to draw on their aid and use them creatively.

Higher archetypes are the pure energies emanating from the Divine, such as Love, Beauty, Peace. Lower, or degraded, archetypes derive from the higher qualities, are often personified and arise from our struggle to understand and come to terms with archetypal forces. Thus Love becomes The Lover; Beauty, The Maiden, Youth, Princess or Prince; Peace, The Peacemaker.

CLEARING THE CENTRAL COLUMN

Keeping the central column energetically clear is the first rule of chakra work. Each chakra feeds into, and is fed from, this central column. Using the breath to keep the energy free-flowing in this column prevents and heals chakra blockages and brings a new balance and vitality to life. Chakric energies need to move easily both upwards and downwards through your body. The following exercises are crucial in establishing this movement and in clearing the central column. They should be used as a preparation for meditation and healing and before doing any of the other exercises in this book. This form of breathing will subsequently be referred to as 'central column breathing'.

Exercise 1
Central Column Breathing

Stand or sit with your spine straight and your body balanced. Do not cross your legs if you are sitting in a chair, or your ankles if you are sitting on the floor, unless you are in the lotus position or a 'cross-legged' posture.

- Begin by being aware of the rhythm of your breathing and letting it slow down.
- Now draw the breath in as though it comes from just above the crown of your head; draw it down through the centre of your body. Change to the out-breath at a point which feels natural for you and breathe out as though right down and through your legs and into the earth. (The breath will not go down through your legs if you are in a cross-legged or lotus position but these postures automatically balance energies in the body and chakras.) Breathe in this way about five times (i.e. five in/out breaths = one sequence).
- Now, on the alternate breath sequence, begin to breathe up from the earth, through the centre of your body, letting the out-breath go out through the crown of your head.
- Continue to breathe in this way, without straining or forcing, for about five minutes. Always end on the downward breath sequence, repeating it in this direction more than once if you wish.
- Feel the balance of your body, resume normal breathing and pause for a few moments before meditating, proceeding to a guided journey or chakra exercise, or returning to your everyday tasks.

Exercise 2
Visualization for the Central Column

If the weather is favourable and there is a suitable tree that you know, it is good to do this exercise with your back against it and your bare feet on the earth. If this is not possible, follow the posture instructions given for Exercise 1.

- Begin by being aware of your breathing rhythm; let it steady and perhaps slow down a little.
- Visualize yourself as a tree. Your branches stretch out above, your roots stretch deeply into the earth, your trunk is straight and strong. You are nurtured by the four elements. The sun (fire) warms you and the air refreshes you. Your roots are in the earth and they seek the underground streams, sources of living water.
- Breathe in through your branches, from the elements of air and sun; take the breath right down through your trunk and breathe out strongly into your roots, into the earth and the streams of living water.
- Breathe in now from the earth and the living water. Bring the breath up, through your roots, through your trunk, into your branches, and breathe out into the elements of air and sun.
- Repeat these two breath sequences for five to ten minutes. Gradually let the visualization fade. Feel your feet firmly on the ground and your own space all around you. Now proceed, with a sense of centredness, to chakra work, meditation or your normal activities.

Chapter 2

Being Here:
Finding a Sense of Purpose

Key Issues: Incarnation, Purpose and Choice
Chakra Pair: Root and Crown
Archetypes: The Sun, the Moon and the Stars

This chapter will help you to:
- be more in tune with incarnation
- be more aware of the elements
- prepare for and face life changes
- gain a better understanding of your life's spiritual purpose
- learn about the meaning and purpose of life on earth

AREAS OF INFLUENCE

The Root Chakra

Location Perineum (the area midway between the anus and the genitals). The petals face downwards, between the legs; the stem faces upwards into the central column and is naturally and healthily slightly open.

Colours Red; Brown; Mauve
Key Words Rootedness, Incarnation, Acceptance, Self-Preservation, Concept
Developmental Age 0–3/5 years
Element Earth
Sense Smell
Body Physical
Glandular Connection Gonads
Quietening Fragrances Cedarwood, Patchouli
Stimulating Fragrances Musk, Lavender, Hyacinth
Crystals and Gemstones Smoky Quartz, Garnet, Alexandrite, Ruby, Agate Bloodstone, Onyx, Tiger's Eye, Rose Quartz

Prayer or Affirmation

Through incarnation may spirit be brought into matter. Through rootedness may life-force be recharged and exchanged. We acknowledge wholeness and seek to gain and to reflect acceptance.

The Crown Chakra

Location At the top of the head with myriad petals (the thousand-petalled lotus) facing upwards and a stem going down into the central column
Colours Violet, White, Gold
Key Words Soul, Surrender, Release, Incoming Will
Element Magnetum
Body Soul, Ketheric or Causal
Glandular Connection Pituitary
Quietening Fragrances Rosemary, Bergamot
Stimulating Fragrances Violet, Amber
Crystals and Gemstones Diamond, White Tourmaline, White Jade, Snowy Quartz, Celestite

Prayer or Affirmation

Through surrender and release let the incoming will be truly the will of God working within us and through us, leading us increasingly to knowledge of mystical union and mystical marriage.

ROOT AND CROWN AS A CHAKRA PAIR

The breathing exercise central column also establishes the fundamental link between the root and crown chakras.

The developmental stage for the root chakra is from birth to 3/5 years. This does not mean that a baby only has a root chakra. The seven-layered energetic body of which the chakras form a major part is essential to life itself. A baby has a full chakra system, yet the early months and years vitally affect the functioning and potential of the root chakra. If these years contain all that the baby needs, and are full of love and nurturing, then the root chakra flourishes and the foundations for later strengths are fully laid.

Clairvoyantly seen, the root chakra is the simplest of them all. Its petals face downwards, from the perineum area into the earth and, ideally, are always at least partially open. The stem goes up into the central column. A direct upward flow of energy from the root, through the central column into the open stem and petals of the crown, and an answering flow from the crown, down the central column, through the stem of the root, out through its petals, into the earth, establish a vital interconnection. A question to ask yourself, linked to the sense connection of the root chakra, is: 'How do I smell the world and how does the world smell me?'

The root is the slowest and the crown the fastest in the chakra team in terms of movement and colour vibration. The crown has been described as 'the thousand-petalled lotus'. When balanced and healthy it is always open, moving and oscillating with high intensity. Red (root) has the slowest vibration in the colour spectrum and violet (crown) the highest.

The crown chakra is the gateway through which the energy of the soul and the higher self stream into our spiritual consciousness and inspire our incarnation. These energies have to be earthed and the root chakra is the complementary gateway through which this happens.

KEY ISSUES

The key life issues affected by the pairing between root and crown chakras at the spiritual level are incarnation, purpose and choice.

Incarnation

The word 'incarnation' literally means 'embodiment'. It therefore covers all the issues around the process of taking on a body, being born and finding our place in life. In addition to the spiritual implications there are emotional and physical factors to be considered.

The search for a deeper meaning to life leads us inevitably to the need for spiritual models or hypotheses. We need a *spiritual*, rather than a specifically *religious*, language to enable philosophical discussion and a wider comprehension. Chakras, as previously explained, derive their names from Sanskrit and Eastern spiritual philosophies, and so the context and function of each chakra naturally tends to be described using terms of mainly Eastern origin. Alongside 'incarnation' we need to use words like 'reincarnation', 'karma', 'the higher self', 'soul', 'spirit', 'destiny' and 'evolution', in order to widen our understanding of why and how we came to be here.

Gildas has summarized some of these concepts. He tells us that the impulse to incarnate comes from the soul, which is beyond the being in human form.

The soul, whose wisdom and experience is gathered by the overseeing intelligence known as the higher self, is intent on evolving into wholeness or perfection. Many lifetimes are needed for evolution and in each lifetime we become progressively more aware of the need for communion with our souls and for greater understanding of our purpose.

The spirit is the pure, animating, essence of being and is fully present within each one of us in every incarnation. The soul, however, remains on a different plane of consciousness, overseeing the process of evolution.

The goal of evolution is enlightenment, perfection or wholeness – a state of being in which we are beyond attachment and the limitations of the finite mind, no longer have any need to incarnate, and are journeying towards union with the Divine Source of All Being.

The pitfalls of the learning process mean that karma, the spiritual law of cause and effect, is activated (see also Glossary).

From karma comes the concept of reincarnation – or many lifetimes – in which to gain experience and learn the consequences of misuse or misinterpretation of the Divine Principles.

The Divine Principles (or higher archetypes) are pure, abstract forces affecting and motivating us all the time. As we interpret them so we name them: Love, Justice, Peace, Beauty, Harmony, Power, Service, Wholeness and Perfection. We struggle to live by these principles and, in order to understand them, we break them down into component parts and archetypes are created (such as the twenty-two archetypes in the major arcana of Tarot, see page 32 and Glossary).

The higher self takes an overview before and after each incarnation in order to assess progress, make choices, open opportunities or provide specific learning situations relevant to the soul's evolution. Consequently, each incarnating being carries the seeds of destiny.

Purpose

Destiny is the sum total of the choices made by the higher self for a particular incarnation. It includes the evolutionary lessons to be learned, the karma to be repaid, the imbalances to be rectified and the service we may elect to give to humanity or the earth. Our higher selves also endeavour to involve us particularly with one or more of the Divine Principles or archetypal themes. When we reach an understanding of the archetypal umbrella under which we live, we can work more consciously towards evolution and spiritual fulfilment.

Each of us incarnates with an 'incoming will to. . . ' – or under the influence of an overlighting angel. When we learn to live in harmony with this, the whole of life becomes more congruent. Thus our incoming will may urge us to teach, to learn, to heal, to create beauty or harmony, to govern, to be involved with justice or peace, to serve, to explore, to philosophize, to wield power, to bring love. . .

Knowing, identifying and acknowledging our overall 'will to . . .' or life theme, and making contact with our overlighting angel, is an important issue. (See Exercise 4, page 37). Many of us long to be relieved of the burden of choice. 'If only someone would tell me what I should be doing then I could get on and do it' is a plea which I constantly hear in my work. It is not as simple as this.

Choice

Even when we feel we have identified our incoming will or key word, or made creative contact with our overlighting angel, we still need to acknowledge that each area of possibility is a wide umbrella. We still need to make choices, find motivation and create our lives.

Many people who come for personal consultations with my discarnate guide, Gildas, ask the question: 'What is my life purpose?' Usually Gildas can see the incoming flow from the higher self and even contact the overlighting angel. He can then interpret and communicate the main key or task words for the present incarnation. He also firmly points out that, for each one of us, the overall spiritual purpose of life is evolution. In order to evolve we need experience and therefore every day, every hour and every minute of our lives is an accomplishment of life purpose. The main task is to become more conscious of ourselves and of the experiences we are having, in order to activate our power of choice. For many of us it is exactly this power which we find so formidable. How do we choose? What if we make the wrong choice?

Gildas informs us that there *are* no wrong choices. We agonize unnecessarily over some life decisions, telling ourselves that there must be a right or wrong direction to take at each of life's crossroads. Sometimes we stay stuck at the crossroads, unable to read the signs or make a decision about which way to turn. Influenced, as we are, by the Christian ethic (as interpreted by the Church), we tend to think that self-sacrifice and choosing the most difficult path must somehow be more virtuous than treading the way of true joy and inner fulfilment. We see God, guides, higher selves, angels and spiritual helpers as demanding killjoys and imagine that the most effective lessons can only be learned through pain and suffering. Unless the medicine tastes nasty we think it can't be doing any good! However, once we understand more of the mechanisms of the higher self, decisions and choices can be made more freely and creatively. We are often our own hardest taskmasters.

Gildas says:

Choice is a necessary part of life in earth incarnation. But in the widest sense there are no wrong choices. Before you come into incarnation your higher self has made selections which ensure that the scene for evolutionary experience is set. The historical time and culture for your incarnation are chosen, as is your initial social milieu. Children choose their parents. Parents choose their children. Gender, body type and mental orientation are also decided before physical conception takes place. Even the astrological influences at the moment of birth are chosen and directed.

In this way your lives are circumscribed. Certain choices will be impossible for the incarnate self to make, whilst any choice which is within the realms of possibility will lead to valuable experience which your soul still needs for evolution. Therefore each time you are at a crossroads different but *equally valuable* experiences are available whichever direction you take. It is then for you, in your incarnate personality, to decide which direction will bring you the most fulfilment and how much or how little you want to stretch yourself. Higher selves want each being in incarnation to be self-actualizing [see Glossary] but no one expects you to jump through hoops. All guides and advisers on this side of life hope that you will find joy and consciousness in incarnation and in connection with the earth and what it has to offer.

The only wrong choices come when, with full conscious-ness, you turn to the dark or evil side of life and create disharmony or wilful harm. The basic law of human nature is harmlessness. There are multiple complexities associated with the honouring of this law but if you try to live by it to the extent of your conscious awareness at any given moment then wrong choices are not part of the picture. Embrace life's opportunities with confidence, neither fear change, nor be addicted to it for its own sake, and you will steer a true course through evolutionary opportunities and concerns.

HIGHER ARCHETYPES AND THE INCOMING WILL

A fuller list of key words which apply to the incoming will or which describe the nature of the overlighting angel is derived from the list of Divine Principles or archetypes of higher qualities. No suggested list can be comprehensive. We need to find the key word which really motivates and speaks to us at a personal level. This means that any given list will have room within it for creativity. There will always be additional words close to the meaning of others which are more pertinent or meaningful to a particular individual.

For some, like John (see case study, page 29), the key word will be more straightforward and easily related to the basic list of archetypal higher qualities. For others it will be more elusive or subtle, requiring considerable thought or meditation in order to arrive at the word which really encapsulates or enlivens the inner sense of life purpose. Here, I give some suggested lists of words arising from each of the archetypes of higher qualities, which may help you in your search to understand your incoming will and to have clearer contact with your over-lighting angel of purpose. (see also Exercise 4, page 37). Some words appear in more than one list as the archetypes can engender similar qualities. Yet it is subtly, but importantly, different to work with creativity under the archetype of love than to work with creativity under the archetype of power. Each has its place; one is not better than the other, but they fulfil a different purpose.

From the higher archetype of **Love** come: love of God, love of others, self-sacrifice, tenderness, mothering, nurturing, caring, creativity, dedication, vocation, commitment, healing, love of earth and growing things, love of animals, conservation, transformation, giving, contentment.

From the higher archetype of **Justice** come: equality, fairness, administration, law, order, guardianship, authority, leadership, reform, social conscience, politics, mitigation, arbitration, warriorship, human rights, debate, caring, idealism.

From the higher archetype of **Peace** come: peace-making, warriorship, arbitration, citizenship, defence, guardianship, healing, planning, order, freedom, relating, union, humanitarianism, safety, prayer, meditation, quietude.

From the higher archetype of **Beauty** come: preservation, creativity, shaping, artistry, skill, observation, grace, transformation, appreciation, colour, design, architecture, building, vision, assessment, perspective, awareness.

From the higher archetype of **Harmony** come: music, creativity, peace-making, dance, art, colour, design, symmetry, arbitration, counselling, inner searching, healing, friendship, empathy, rhythm, understanding, tolerance.

From the higher archetype of **Power** come: rulership, leadership, teaching, priesthood, government, self-empowerment, empowerment of others, self-actualization (see also Glossary), ambition, initiating, competitiveness, acquisition, responsibility, direction, inspiration, vision, hope, dedication, idealism, belief, courage, confidence, law and order, competence.

From the higher archetype of **Service** come: dedication, purpose, serving others, responsibility, administration, law and order, transformation, transmutation, healing, counselling, giving, self-sacrifice, social conscience, belief, social reform, improvement, idealism, patriotism, humanitarianism, love of others.

From the higher archetype of **Wholeness** come: self-growth, equality, balance, inclusiveness, healing, perception, blending, acceptance, seeking, exploration, assimilation, completion, vision, tolerance, breadth of knowledge, symbolism, creativity.

From the higher archetype of **Perfection** come: idealism, God consciousness, dedication, striving, healing, endeavour, vision, stoicism, industriousness, seeking the highest, goodness, belief, setting standards, aims, goal-setting, confidence, focus, advising, leadership, artistry, worth, conservation, preservation, following a prescribed path closely, application, diligence.

I have tried to avoid using words which have any negative connotations but, of course, almost anything which gets out of proportion can be seen as negative. All these aspects, in proportion and context, have positive and balanced applications.

Discovering the key archetypes and words which give you a

clearer sense of your incoming will or overlighting angel will not always immediately lead you to the perfect study, work or career. But they will give you a clearer sense of why you are here and a fuller understanding of the purposes of your higher self. Any combination of the key words can be applied to a variety of careers and will strengthen you in the style with which you approach the work you have chosen or from which, at present, there is no way out.

We are a *doing*-orientated society. Care must be taken to ensure that the key words are also considered in relationship to work or lifestyles which are more *being*-orientated. Creating and maintaining a beautiful home or garden and mothering children are, at one level, very active and demanding tasks, yet it is the happy homemaker's quality of being which deeply touches others. Some people also know that the actual nature of the work they do is less important than the quality of being which they bring to it. Some people learn to *be* through *doing* – others learn to *do* through *being*.

Case Study: Finding Your Incoming Will

John, in his early forties, was following a successful career as a teacher. He was a well-respected departmental head in a large secondary school. To all appearances he seemed to be the epitome of the career teacher, on the brink of further promotions and success. He was happily married to Ursula, also a teacher, who had recently become head of a local village school. They had a comfortable home and their son and daughter were both doing well at university. To the onlooker, they seemed to have achieved that rounded contentment in life which can be so elusive.

When John made an appointment to see me he had recently become interested in the transpersonal approach to therapy and counselling (see Glossary). He outlined his basic problem as 'disillusionment and loss of direction'. He felt that his life and career had lost their meaning and even wondered if he had ever known real meaning in its deepest sense. He regularly attended services at his local Anglican church but had begun to lose the comfort, solace and inspiration which he had earlier found in conventional worship.

John felt depressed, isolated and at a dead end. Outwardly he was trying to behave as normal but inwardly he was under considerable stress. The idea of changing his career or life direction seemed too awful to contemplate. Ursula and the children were settled and happy. John felt that if *he* changed the whole family would inevitably be adversely affected. He was unwilling to cause a family crisis and disrupt the lives of his loved ones. Furthermore, there was nothing John passionately wanted to do instead of teaching. But, if he remained in this career, he despaired of finding the inner and outer strength to maintain the high standards he had always set for himself and which were now automatically expected of him.

I felt that John was experiencing a spiritual crisis in the widest sense, as well as a degree of mental and physical burnout. This latter state needed to be dealt with at a practical level so that measures could be taken to alleviate or prevent the onset of physical stress symptoms. The long school holidays were not far away but John usually spent the major part of these reviewing previous work and preparing for the next school year. There would be two weeks for a family holiday. This year his student children were breaking from family tradition and had made their own arrangements. John felt that he and Ursula might just stay at home and attend to the garden. But when he had listened to what I had to say about burnout, John said he would seriously consider taking a longer break with Ursula, perhaps abroad, seeing this also as a celebration of her recent promotion.

Having emphasized that the physical needs were important, I then began to talk to John about archetypes of purpose. He felt that he had rather drifted into teaching, since at school he had not wanted to be a doctor, lawyer or priest and, at the time, teaching had seemed the only other alternative. Until recently he had been fulfilled in teaching. Now he found it difficult to maintain momentum but could not see any viable alternative. Somehow his relationship with the archetype of teacher had never been fully forged; he felt swept along by it; that it was in charge of his life and had cut off all other avenues. In some ways he felt he was the victim of the archetype.

In the end, John and Ursula decided to take a month's holiday abroad and, as he left, I asked him to think about teaching as an archetypal umbrella and to see whether any aspects of it excited him more than others. He also agreed to look at the other important umbrella archetypes to discover which seemed most energized for him.

With the start of the new school year John returned to our sessions. His thoughts around archetypes of purpose had proved fruitful. Deep reflection had convinced him that he had not so much drifted into teaching for lack of other choice but that teaching had subtly called him. 'I feel myself to be an educator,' he said. The aspect of teaching which currently excited him most was the work he did with younger teachers, helping them find their feet in their chosen career and supporting the development of their teaching skills and strengths. Whilst reading teaching journals his attention had been drawn to vacancies for lecturers in teacher training. He felt he would need to do some part-time courses before applying for such a post but becoming a trainer of teachers was now his clear goal.

In the interim, giving more lead to the young staff in his school would provide sufficient challenge for him to carry on where he was. He felt that he was forging a new relationship with the archetype of teaching or education, and could avoid becoming its victim in future, drawing on it, instead, for true inspiration and a sense of life purpose. A move into teacher training would be reasonably non-disruptive to the life of his family. He felt revitalized and that his dead end had become a crossroads, with him feeling confident now as to which direction to take.

John continued to come for sessions to discuss the spiritual side of life. He continued to go to church but also practised meditation and read widely in spiritual literature. His view of the universe and the purposes within it changed and widened.

Eighteen months later, when I was only seeing John for infrequent sessions, he phoned to say he had been successful in obtaining a post in teacher training and was full of eager anticipation. Everyone was thrilled for him. He was moving on with their blessing, even though his head and colleagues were sorry to lose such a valued staff member.

THE ARCHETYPES: THE SUN, THE MOON AND THE STARS

Whilst the qualities of love, justice, peace, beauty, harmony, power, service, wholeness and perfection are Divine Principles or archetypes of higher qualities, there are a host of other, more personified archetypes. They are often described as 'primordial images inherited by all'. Jung saw them as universal energy forces affecting each one of us by day and by night. They always represent principles, ideas or forces with which we need to come to terms in the course of life on earth.

The list of twenty-two archetypes covered by the major arcana of Tarot is fairly comprehensive, but there are always others which can be added. Reading the Tarot is a way of discovering which particular archetypes are most affecting our lives at any given time. The twenty-two archetypes of the Tarot major arcana are: the Fool, the Magician, the High Priestess, the Empress, the Emperor, the Hierophant, the Lovers, the Chariot, Strength, the Hermit, the Wheel of Fortune, Justice, the Hanged Man, Death, Temperance, the Devil, the Lightning-

Struck Tower, the Star, the Moon, the Sun, Judgement, the World.

Chakras have archetypal connotations and meanings. In suggesting archetypes for pairs and groups of chakras my aim is to help you gain greater insight into the subtle meanings and wide areas which they cover. Making connections between chakras, colours, gemstones and archetypes offers us a variety of ways of working with each chakra, pair, or group, one of which will seem appropriate to your growth.

The archetypes chosen for the 'Being Here' aspects of the root and crown chakras are: the Sun, the Moon and the Stars.

The Sun

The sun has been selected as an archetype for these chakras because, as it 'dies' and is 'born' again during each 24-hour cycle, it symbolizes death and rebirth.

The astrological glyph (or symbolic sign) for the sun is a dot within a circle. When we let go of old conditioning and find a true sense of purpose, we may need to let a part of ourselves die in order to be reborn. Gildas tells us that the higher self *circumscribes* our free life choices by the conditions it has already selected (see page 26). The dot within the circle is the part of each one of us which says 'I'. When we have explored the circle of choice more fully we can truly say 'I am', feeling confident in greater self-knowledge.

The sun can be seen as the higher self, shining in through the crown, fertilizing, enlivening and awakening the root chakra whose element is earth.

The symbolism of the root chakra is partly connected with the need to put roots deep into the earth so that the tree of the self may grow strong, tall, balanced and open its branches to the nurturing of the sun.

In most traditions the sun is the Universal Father, or the symbol for the masculine principle, whereas the moon is a major aspect of the Great Mother and the symbol for the feminine principle. The interaction of these primary principles produces creativity.

Psychologically the sun can represent the conscious, active mind, and the moon the unconscious, dreaming mind.

The Moon

The moon has been chosen as an archetype relating to the crown and root chakras because it represents the receptive, reflective, dreamy, unconscious aspects of ourselves. As we find our place on earth and evolve, these aspects need to be brought to fruition.

Universally, the moon is symbolic of the rhythms and cycles of life. As the moon waxes, wanes and goes into its dark time of withdrawal, it portrays the constant need for that which is unconscious to be brought into the light of awareness.

Reflecting the light of the sun, the moon represents the journey of the incarnate personality as, through the cycles of evolution, it seeks to understand and fulfil the purposes of the higher self.

The Stars

Stars have been selected as the third archetypal symbol of these chakras because stars in the heavens can symbolize our true or ascendant selves, fully in harmony with life and opportunity. They are also the eyes of the night, bringing hope and clarity when we are confused or muddled.

The pole, or north star, gives us direction; when it is identified in the sky we always know our path of travel. Stars are also connected with ancient wisdom. Since they have witnessed the whole history of the universe, they can inspire us to make creative decisions and show us where our true talents lie.

EXERCISES

Exercise 3
Considering Your Body

It is preferable to do this exercise lying down, on the floor, on a bed, or sofa. Make sure that you will be undisturbed, have writing materials at hand, and cover yourself with a rug for greater comfort or to avoid getting cold.

- Be in touch with the rhythm of your breathing. Do not try to change your breath rhythm, just observe it. Let your whole body relax. Starting at your feet and working upwards, be conscious of any physical tensions and breathe them out on the out-breath. On each in-breath, breathe in a sense of warmth and relaxation.
- Begin to make a mental note of, or ask your body to remember, the places where you hold most tension. Is it in your feet, knees, thighs, or the whole of your legs? Your genitals? Buttocks? Abdomen? Lower or upper back? Solar plexus? Rib cage? Arms, elbows, or hands? Shoulders? Neck? Head? Around your eyes? In your mouth, lips, tongue or teeth?
- Know that, throughout the whole of this exploration, with each outbreath you take you will automatically continue to breathe away tensions, and with each in-breath you will continue to breathe in warmth and relaxation.
- For five more minutes continue to be aware of your breathing, thus focusing on the **air** element in your body. Do you naturally breathe deeply or shallowly? Do you breathe relatively quickly or slowly? If you put your hands near the bottom of your ribs can you feel your diaphragm working as you breathe in and out? Feel the air coming in through your nostrils and being taken to your lungs. Imagine your body taking in oxygen, eliminating carbon

dioxide and other toxins, sustaining vital life energy for
you. You can live for only a very short time without
breathing. Appreciate the air you breathe and your body's
automatic function of in-breathing and out-breathing. (If
you want to make any notes before going on to the element
of fire, take a moment to do so and then relax down
again).

- When you are ready, begin to contemplate the element of
  fire in your body. Fire energy keeps you warm, digests and
  metabolizes your food, causes your blood to circulate, is
  your basic energy, your initiative, your 'get up and go';
  brings you light and vision; makes you creative; affects your
  sexuality; and in chakra terms is mostly connected to
  your solar plexus. After five minutes considering the
  element of fire take time to make notes and then relax
  down again as you prepare to reflect upon the element of
  water.

- Our bodies are said to consist of 80–90 percent **water**.
  Imagine the water and fluids in your body. Water works
  to cleanse, to digest, to metabolize, to eliminate. Consider
  your urinary system and the processes of bodily elimination via the water element.

- Blood nourishes and circulates, bringing life to every bodily
  area: if we are wounded and lose too much blood we
  cannot survive; if we suffer from anaemia our energies
  become severely depleted. If you are a woman, ponder
  your menstrual cycle and the part which blood plays in
  gestation and birth.

- After five minutes reflection on the water element, take
  time to make notes and then relax down again as you
  prepare to consider the element of earth.

- **Earth** in the body is bone, muscle, flesh and physical
  substance. What kind of body do you have? Tall? Short?
  Lean? Well-covered? Stocky? Strong? Athletic? Healthy?
  Delicate? Fragile? Energetic? Lethargic?

- Consider the texture of your skin and hair; be aware of

your bones. What do you feel about your body? Does it carry you easily through life? Are you reasonably content with it? Are there improvements you long for? Can you think of your body as a friend or do you need to work on this?

- After five minutes contemplation write down the things you like and the things you dislike about your body. Which list is longer? How easy or difficult is it to admit to the things you like or the things you dislike?

- Having become aware of your body and its elements, reflect on its strengths and imbalances. Make any decisions you feel able to make at this point, as to how you might help to balance the elements in your body. In chakra terms, working with the root chakra helps the earth element; working with the sacral chakra balances the water element; working with the solar plexus aids the fire energy and working with the heart stabilizes the element of air.

- Reflect on the things your body does easily and the things it finds difficult. Ponder on the ways in which your body may be guiding you towards, or away from, certain occupations and interests and how this may reflect guidance or choice from your higher self (see also pages 25–6).

Exercise 4
Contacting Your Overlighting Angel

Make sure that you will be undisturbed, and that you have writing and drawing materials at hand. Sit or lie down for this exercise. Arrange your body symmetrically. Sit cross-legged or in a lotus position if you wish, but otherwise, whether seated on a chair or lying down, do not cross your legs at the knees or ankles. Your head should be in alignment with your spine and well balanced or supported if you are in a sitting position.

- Do the central column breathing exercise
- When are ready to do so, bring your attention into your crown chakra and sense its quality and movement. Imagine, see or visualize the constantly moving thousand-petalled lotus, reflecting the main colours of violet, gold and white. Sense a stream of golden light coming into the centre of the crown lotus from above. This light runs right through this chakra, down the central column and out through the root.
- Endeavour to sense an angelic being from which some of this golden light is streaming. Feel the light expanding around you like a cloak of golden light . . . Let the light penetrate each part, each cell of your body, bringing you warmth, light and healing . . . Ask to be made aware of the important key words for your life and purpose (see pages 25 and 29). Get a feeling of the things in life which feed your creativity and sense of fulfilment . . . Ask for words or symbols which will enable you to be clearer about your sense of purpose in this lifetime . . .
- After five to ten minutes, gradually let the light fade; be fully aware, once more, of your crown chakra; and visualize a cross of light in a circle of light above it as a blessing . . . Thank your overlighting angel and your higher self for their light and wisdom . . . Become aware of your body on the chair or the floor; feel your connection with the earth; and put a cloak of light with a hood around you, thus holding yourself in light so that you are not vulnerable, but also having light to take with you wherever you go.
- Make any notes or drawings which will help you remember anything which you experienced during this meditation. You may need to repeat it several times on different occasions before you get the answers or certainties you are looking for.

Exercise 5
The Archetype of the Sun

Follow the instructions given for Exercise 3 (page 35) about body position and making sure you will be undisturbed. Have drawing and writing materials to hand.

- Be in touch with the rhythm of your breathing, watching each in-breath and each out-breath. Allow yourself to enter a quiet, meditative, inner space.
- Reflect upon the journey of the sun throughout the day and throughout the year. Consider your favourite time of day and your best-loved season of the year. What is the position of the sun at these times?
- A day is born, a day dies, to be followed by a new day . . . Ponder the phases of your life . . . Where are you at present? Have you just made a new start? Is it a flourishing time, with the sun at its zenith? Or are you beginning to feel ready for a rest, a holiday or a rethink? Has something just ended and are you unsure of the rebirth or new beginning? Match where you are in your life to a time of day and reflect on the qualities of this time of day and what it has to offer . . .
- By knowing which season you prefer and matching a season to where you are now symbolically, in your life, you can gain a better understanding of what needs to be done or accepted before your favourite season begins once more.
- When you have finished these considerations, draw the sun meditatively, feeling as deeply as possible what it means to you and to life in general.

Exercise 6
The Archetype of the Moon

Make similar preparations to those suggested for Exercise 3 (page 35).

- Use the rhythm of your breathing to help you enter a meditative inner space . . . In your mind's eye see the moon, shining brightly over the countryside, and surrounded by stars, on a clear night . . . Note what season of the year it may be . . . This is the full moon. As you absorb its silvery light, reflect on the other cycles of the moon: the waning; the dark of the moon; the new crescent and waxing moon; the full moon once more . . .
- Ponder on how events and memories in life are sometimes in full consciousness and later become less conscious or forgotten, as in the waning and dark phases of the moon . . . Remember the joy of a new idea or a new passion, at first, like the new moon, growing into its full strength, and then waning again . . . Consider how your conscious and unconscious minds interact, and how dreams and meditations may sometimes bring useful material from the unconscious into form, memory or inspiration, feeding creativity and reminding you of the richness you carry within . . .
- As you meditatively draw a picture of the moon, ask yourself whether you need to attend more to your dreams? Do you need more time for yourself, for withdrawal or meditation?
- Reflect on the cycles of the moon as phases of incarnation, reincarnation and evolution . . . Endeavour to get a sense of what might have gone before, to place you where you are now in the evolutionary and karmic cycle . . .

Exercise 7
The Archetype of the Stars

Make initial preparations as for Exercise 3 (page 35).

- Use the rhythm of your breath to help you enter your quiet,
  inner, meditative space . . . Find yourself, once more,
  contemplating a night-time scene, with the stars shining
  very clearly in the sky . . . Pick out the north, or pole
  star . . . Imagine yourself travelling to that star on a beam
  of light . . . When you have reached the star, look down
  upon the earth and get a sense of the direction you are at
  present facing and the direction in which you perhaps
  need to travel . . . Is the same path illuminated by your star?
  Is a slight change of direction indicated? Does the light
  of the star show a complete change of direction as being
  possible or viable for you?
- Reflect on how it feels to be a star in the ascendant,
  knowing your course and place in the universe . . .
- As you draw the stars in the sky, and the north star shining
  on your direction, consider the times in your life when
  you have really felt yourself to be on course, like a star in
  the sky. What are the ingredients you need to have around
  you in order to feel fulfilled? Which of these ingredients
  are significantly present or missing now?

THE COLOURS

The main colours for the root chakra are red, brown and
mauve.

On the positive side, red is a colour associated with warmth,
action and growth. On the negative side, it can be associated
with anger, danger or emergency.

Red is a good healing colour for bones, muscles and the tissues of the body, though it is wise to modify it from a bright or cardinal red to a more gentle, rich, rosy red for healing.

Positively, brown is an earthy colour: fertile, fecund and gestating. Negatively, it can be depressive, static or limiting.

The positive attributes of mauve are coolness, peacefulness and purification. On its negative side it can be too cold, indefinite, sterile and disturbing.

Mauve is the colour from the root which most links with the crown centre, since violet is a deeper and higher vibrational development of mauve.

The main colours for the crown are violet, white and gold.

On the positive side, violet is warm, stimulating, regal, majestic, awakening of dormant spirituality and inspiring of vision. On the negative side, it can be distancing, negatively superior, antagonistic and over-stimulating.

Positively, white is pure, reflective, symbolic of both innocence and perfection, yang, or of the masculine principle. Negatively, it can signify cowardice, incomprehension, lack of depth and blankness.

In the technical sense white and black are not colours at all. White reflects all colours and black absorbs them all.

Gold, at the crown, is pure metallic gold. Positively, it is attainment, perfection, the sun, purity, value, integrity. Negatively, it may be seen as signifying false attachment, worldliness, false values, seduction and being dazzled or confused.

Exercise 8
Using the Colours

It would help to have a box of bright pastels for this and other exercises in this book. The ability of pastels to blend enables the greatest range of colours to be explored.

The colours as seen in the chakras are full of light and

vitality. They appear as stained glass does when sunlight passes through it.

- Consider these colours and meditatively draw their many shades and tones. As you draw, sense the tones or shades which are most attractive to you.
- Linking the root and crown chakras is particularly helped by drawing the tone scale from brightest cardinal red through to the bright violet of an African violet blossom.
- Use these colours to heal your root and crown chakras by breathing them in through the petals and out through the stems. Breathe each colour of your choice into the appropriate chakra for five breath sequences as follows. Draw the colour in through the petals on the in-breath, hold the colour in the centre of the chakra (where it interpenetrates with the physical body) for a count of three, and then breathe it out through the stem. (This equals one breath sequence.)

THE FRAGRANCES

If you are anxious about your purpose in life and about incarnation itself, if you find difficulty in putting down roots and dealing with the practical issues of life, if you often feel angry at the circumstances of your incarnation or about your body, then your root and crown chakras need the stimulating fragrances of musk, lavender or hyacinth for the root and violet and amber for the crown.

If you are over-diligent about your purpose in life and continually give yourself to others, if you find it difficult to allow yourself comfort and nurturing, then your crown chakra needs the quietening fragrances of rosemary and bergamot and your root needs the stimulating ones of musk, lavender and hyacinth.

If you are over-concerned about your earthly surroundings, always cleaning things which are already spotless, concerned with over-orderliness, living an immaculate life but often feeling uncomfortable with the demands it makes, then your root chakra needs the quietening fragrances of cedarwood and patchouli.

These quietening fragrances for the root chakra can also help anorexia and compulsive eating if used together with the quietening fragrances, for the solar plexus, of vetivert and rose. Quietening fragrances for the root can ease obsessional or compulsive behaviour patterns when used together with the quietening fragrances for the sacral chakra which are musk and amber.

You do not have to use all the fragrances for any one chakra or intention. You can choose the most compatible for you. Blend them together or use them alternately (see page 43 for more instructions and suggestions on how to work with fragrances).

THE CRYSTALS

The Glossary suggests methods for the full cleaning of crystals, but before you use a crystal for an exercise hold it under cold running water for a few moments and then dry it on a natural fibre cloth.

You do not need to do anything elaborate with a crystal in order to obtain its benefits. Just hold or examine it, have it in your environment where you can readily see it, put it near your bed, hold it during meditation, have it with you in your car, or wrap it in silk and take it with you in your pocket wherever you go. Use only one or two crystals at a time as you focus on a particular life improvement or enhancement you wish to make.

To strengthen your sense of contentment or acceptance at

being incarnate, and to link your root and crown chakras, select from the following crystals:

Onyx To bring strength and stamina and to heal the stresses which come from worldly responsibilities.

Tiger's Eye To encourage the making of creative choices. To create unity between your higher and lower selves. To bring strength for meeting life challenges.

Snowy Quartz To heal any sense of reluctance about being incarnate and to strengthen your relationship with your higher self.

Celestite For help with meditation in general and for making contact with your overlighting angel in particular.

PRAYERS OR AFFIRMATIONS

A prayer or affirmation for the root chakra is given on page 20 and for the crown on page 21.

To use the words given as an affirmation, say or read them through three times in succession two or three times daily.

To use the words as a prayer, read them through slowly, meditating a little after each phrase. Ask the angels of virtue, who deal with the energy of prayer, to take your prayer to the Divine Source and to bring an answering flow from the Source into your life. (For more on angels, see *The River of Life* and *Working With Guides and Angels* in the Bibliography.)

Chapter 3

Body of Evidence:
Healing Physical Ailments

Key Issues: The Body and its Healing Needs

Chakra Pair: Root and Crown

Archetype: Healing

This chapter will help you to:
- better understand and accept your body and your gender
- know that your body helps you to find your purpose and destiny in life
- understand something of the wisdom of dis-ease and work with symbols for self-healing

---

AREAS OF INFLUENCE

For lists of the areas of influence of the root and crown chakras see pages 19–21.

THE ROOT CHAKRA AND THE PHYSICAL BODY

Our auras, or subtle energy fields, surround and interpenetrate our physical bodies. Each chakra, in relation to the aura, enables us to connect with a particular energy level, layer, plane, vibration or body. The six energy planes or bodies which exist beyond the material and physical are termed 'subtle'. Clairvoyants, sensitives, healers, and those who work to develop greater spiritual awareness become more and more alert to the subtle fields and the way they reflect what may be happening, or what is about to happen, at the physical and emotional levels. Healing often has to come through the subtle bodies before it can manifest in the physical, which is why many healers work, at least partly, in the aura, without laying their hands directly on the physical body.

The root chakra connects directly to the physical body and the material plane. As we saw in Chapter 2 (pages 21–22), there is a strong interaction between the crown chakra (seat of the higher self) and the root chakra (seat of the energies of embodiment). Choices made by the higher self manifest in the physical body, giving it aptitudes, gifts and limitations. The other chakras have connections to the emotional, glandular and biochemic systems of the physical body but it is the link between crown and root chakras which most fully determines basic physical endowment (see also page 25).

THE COMPULSION TO CONFORM

We can be healed 'into' ourselves and our highest physical functioning but many basic strengths or inherent weaknesses have, to a large extent, to be accepted, understood and used in the shaping of our lives. Our mental and intellectual faculties play a strong part in determining the scope of outlets for us within our civilization but the body we inhabit, the outer shell, is immediately visible. First impressions can be very powerful and the way we appear can determine many implicit, as well as explicit, factors in the ever-important business of acceptance or rejection by our own kind.

Our society has a puzzling tendency to seek conformity and to set standards of beauty and excellence whilst affirming that each human being is unique. The seeking and upholding of a norm is also largely in direct opposition to theories of karmic learning and evolution through many lifetimes. Having the perfect body can seem to be more important than the quality of one's spirit. Human beings can be very cruel to those who deviate from the physical or mental norm, though in some instances they may assume that such individuals are endowed with special powers.

In some societies or historical eras – especially the Middle Ages in Europe – people have seen 'handicapped', 'misshapen' or mentally 'impaired' humans as objects of fear. They were often thought to have been touched by the devil (potentially inhabited by, and capable of, evil). In societies with a shamanic tradition (see Glossary), those who are born with, or develop some 'abnormality', may be chosen as potential healers, spiritual workers, or dreamers for the tribe.

Handicapped, disabled, or, in the now politically correct terminology, 'challenged', individuals can be set apart, prejudged and condemned to loneliness or self-doubt which goes far beyond the physical. Even being regarded as 'special' can be a burden and limitation.

As teenagers, most of us, though roughly conforming to the 'norm', go through excruciatingly painful doubts about our physical endowments and attributes. We agonize over details such as the length and width of our trousers or skirts, and are desperate to be part of the 'in' group.

Are physical characteristics unfair accidents of genetics and birth? Is 'God' an unfairly selective Creator? Or do our bodies carry some more refined message and meaning?

When we come to believe in karma and evolution through

many lifetimes, these vagaries and apparent shifts of fortune no longer need to be seen as 'unfair' or as meted out by a judgmental and selective Creator. Existential diversity is central to the laws of cause and effect. In our higher selves we actively choose a pre-incarnational focus towards specific areas of learning experience intended to allow us to redress imbalances from other lifetimes.

GENDER

Below, Gildas states that the basic starting consciousness of your individual soul at the commencement of evolution is either yin (feminine principle) or yang (masculine principle). Yet a yin spark can, and, according to esoteric theory, must, also have incarnations as a man, and a yang spark as a woman. This is so that we can encompass the whole spectrum of experience and to enable us to learn about the nature of the divine principles from the joining of which all creativity must proceed.

It follows that one of the major decisions for each incarnation is our choice of gender. In different historical times or cultures, and often according to social milieu, the advantages and disadvantages of being born male or female may change and assume varying significance. At the immediate family level, many of my clients have found their self-worth and even sexual identity has been affected because their parents would have preferred a child of the opposite sex.

As the dysfunctional family of humanity struggles towards mindfulness and integration, the high-profile issues of our times are those of gender, race, colour and creed. Our personal, soul level, choice of gender and the issues which it arouses, relates to life purpose, karma and evolution (see pages 22–6).

We can learn much from reflecting on how we feel about being male/female; how at home we find ourselves to be in a male/female body; how we respond to the demands, expectations or prejudices of society towards those who are male/female; how we respond to, or feel about, the opposite sex, both on an individual basis and as a role model; how comfortable we feel with our sexuality; how we choose to express ourselves sexually; our predisposition or bias towards issues or practice of homosexuality – and many more questions.

Gildas, speaking in similar terms to many other guides, tells us:

> A human soul is a spark which splits off from the Source and chooses human incarnation as its destiny. As it begins its journey of evolution, which will, eventually, lead it back to the Source, the spark partially splits once more. The yin, or feminine of its essence, splits from the yang or masculine. These two essences will take different but complementary and inter-dependent journeys. Each part is like a stem joined at the root or like two strands on a necklace joined at the fastening. Each flower which each stem produces will represent an incarnation. The beads on each strand of the necklace represent opportunities for incarnation. Although, basically, one stem or strand is yin and the other yang, this does not mean that the flowers from the yin stem or beads from the yin strand will always undergo or choose feminine incarnation, nor will those from the yang essence always take on a masculine body – but, at the deepest level, they will carry either a stronger yin or stronger yang, imprint.
>
> The main divine principle is that of creation. Yin and yang energies interacting together bring about the birth of the new. Part of the purpose of evolution for human beings is to understand, experience, and therefore use in a balanced way, these sacred and divine energies. The taking on of a gender is one of the ways in which this learning happens. Since each stem or strand is slanted towards one principle or the other, and since it is possible for twin souls and soul aspects to meet in incarnation

bearing the same gender, homosexuality takes on a different connotation. These things are part of experience, part of exploration, not manifestations which need to be judged or categorically ruled as abnormal, unnatural or dangerous. When a person, on their journey through life, understands that they and others need all kinds of experience, then a broad-based compassion and tolerance develops more easily [see Chapter 6, page 132, for more on twin souls].

The overall purpose of evolution is for the soul to reunite in full consciousness with the Source of All Being. Humanity has chosen the path of knowledge. Unless all experience has been explored and understood, the journey back to the Source cannot be complete. As experience builds, clearer choices can be made. The love impulse which fundamentally governs the universal patterns does not allow the untried and untested to plunge into incarnations which are full of complex difficulties and horrors. Gradually the strand on which the beads are threaded, or the stem which nurtures the flowers, will take a more efficient part in choosing those incarnations most valuable to its continued evolution. The force which is known as karma or 'cause and effect' becomes active.

A personality bead or flower goes into incarnation, lives out its lifespan and dies. In the between-life state which takes place on the astral plane, personality bead and soul thread consider the scope of experience gained and assess all aspects of the harvest which has been reaped. It is on the basis of this assessment that the next life is chosen. A new personality bead prepares to incarnate. Its first brief will be to continue to broaden the scope of experience but it will also carry the knowledge that certain things which may have been out of balance because of choices made during incarnation by the previous bead, need to be rectified or redeemed. The incarnating being, then, will carry a motivation to avoid some types of experience, to embrace others and to confront others.

The choice of historical time, social standing, type of body, parents and siblings will have been made by the higher self to expedite the purposes and tasks of the incarnating being. This includes awareness of other higher selves sending personality beads or flowers into incarnation at a similar time. There may be agreement about helping each other with lessons to be learned or experience to be gained. Where there is a group soul purpose, this will be taken into account so that members of the same group or family can facilitate the group learning process by incarnating together [see also Chapter 4, page 84, for more about group and family karma].

The higher selves making these plans might be seen as actors in the wings of a stage considering the parts they will play, and the interaction they will have, when they actually walk on to the stage. As well as being a personal endeavour and responsibility, evolution is a collective journey.

DISABILITY

We may still ask: 'Why does anyone *choose* to incarnate with a less than perfect, less than optimally functioning physical body?'

Guides and spiritual teachers tend to give the following answers: 'In order to experience and redeem the sort of suffering which has been meted out to others by another personality bead in a previous lifetime'; 'To teach others the compassion a previous bead on your stem lacked'; To make your soul stem more aware and respectful of the physical body rather than taking it for granted'; 'In order to learn the lesson of humility'; 'To compensate for the hedonism or false vanity of another lifetime'; or 'To focus this present lifetime more specifically towards the lessons to be learned and the tasks to be fulfilled'.

If we over-identify with previous lifetimes we can either carry a heavy burden of guilt or suffer from hubris. It is important to remember that it was not I, as I am now, who was physically violent to others in the Middle Ages. Neither was it I, as I am now, who was a wise alchemist in ancient Persia. These were other flowers or beads on the soul stem or thread. I may have access to some of the wisdom gained by that alchemist, but the journey of evolution is not linear and hierarchical. As each personality bead manifests, it may or may not consciously carry past attributes. Sometimes, if we have experienced what it is to be wise, we may need to balance up by experiencing what it is to be foolish. Since *all* experience is necessary to evolution, a gentle incarnation followed by a more violent one can also have a place in the rich tapestry which we can only ever partially comprehend with the finite mind.

The crown chakra helps us to be more in touch with the higher self (see also Glossary) and its intentions and support for the present incarnation. The root chakra gives us the strength to be fully in our physical bodies, to love them for their gifts *and* their limitations, to love the earth and to be fully embodied and present on it. These are among the most important lessons of any incarnation. Understanding and accepting the body we have incarnated into is essential. The following personal story may help to make some of these points clearer and more tangible.

Case Study: Accepting and Loving Your Body

I was born with very limited sight in my right eye but this was not fully diagnosed until I was twelve, by which time I was also very short-sighted in my left eye. In my early years at school my right eye was thought to be 'lazy' and my left, seeing, eye was patched in order to make the right one work. I identified with my right eye and thought that *I* must be lazy or wrong in some way when the patching treatment did not work. With my seeing eye patched, I was virtually blind and so retreated more and more into my own inner world which was already very clear, rich and satisfying.

Partly because of my sight, my body movements were never well synchronized. I longed to be good at sports, gym, ball games and physical feats. I was puzzled that I was unable to achieve the bodily and hand/eye coordination required. I loved animals and yearned to ride horses well but had no natural aptitude. I persisted with trying to fulfil this dream until my late thirties and now carry the scars of dangerous falls. In my dreams I could compete with the most lithe of athletes and ride the wildest of horses.

I have never had any difficulty in meditating or with subtle vision. In this sense I sit lightly upon the earth, yet my physical body is heavy. Carrying too much weight is a constant problem. Although I have often found it difficult to understand why my higher self chose this body, I have gradually accepted that the vivid scenery of some of my dreams of physical prowess belongs to past lives of other beads on my soul stem. My soul stem has already stored this experience. In this lifetime I have needed to look within and develop my inner vision. If I had the body and physical skills of my dreams, I would be riding wild horses, climbing mountains, running races and canoeing down rivers. My life task for this incarnation does not include these things.

I have not found it easy to be on earth. Putting down roots and committing to staying in one place for a lengthy period of time is difficult. I now understand that part of the heaviness of my body is to hold me down and to help me to know earth and substance by having it to deal with in my embodiment.

I have interpreted the lessons for this incarnation which are governed by my body to be:

– Developing a vivid inner world.

- Having clearer subtle sight than outer sight.
- Using these gifts as part of my service to others and teaching others how to develop them.
- Remaining earthed and grounded, so that spirituality is not experienced as something apart from, or rejecting of earth but as an instrument to enhance life on earth and the love of it.
- Not getting diverted from the particular experience which it is my task to take back to my soul thread.

Learning to accept without harbouring resentment is a prime factor in the self-healing process. At fourteen, I was in turmoil about my inner life and my experience of Gildas which had been there as far back as I could remember. Eye specialists feared I might go blind. At nineteen I met Dr Mary Swainson, a Jungian therapist with esoteric and spiritual training. She helped me to see my subtle abilities as a gift. As I did so, my eyesight stabilized and, though I shall always wear spectacles or contact lenses, has never again been the subject of over-concern. My greatest physical weakness or abnormality thus revealed to me my richest gifts, and enabled me to find my greatest strength.

Some lessons take longer! Now, in my sixtieth year, I think and hope that I am coming to terms with my rooting problem. I have also learned to respect and love my body as it is and to appreciate the quality of stamina it has always given me. As this happens, my sense is that some of my body weight may drop away, whereas before, it has always persisted. Strangely, at this point, it is no longer of great importance to me whether the weight shifts or not – but this recognition or acceptance is also one of the intrinsic lessons my body has been able to teach me.

ACCEPTANCE

It is often so! When we stop fighting and the personality or 'little ego' ceases rebelling, physical healing miracles are no longer required or may spontaneously happen where there seemed to be no hope before.

Beyond the size, nature, shape, limitations and gifts of our physical bodies, lie strengths or weaknesses in particular bodily systems. Though other chakras are linked to the body's biochemic constitution, the crown remains the place of choice and the root the place of manifestation and embodiment. When crown and root chakras work in harmony together there is a strong foundation from which understanding and healing can flow.

Gildas gives us 'Acceptance' as one of the key words for spiritual growth. He does not mean that our attitude should be passive. This key word can teach us that graceful acceptance of a status quo will release blockages and enable creativity. Through active acceptance we learn to work more skilfully with the basic materials and gifts that are to hand instead of yearning for something other. In short, we learn to accept and value ourselves.

Acceptance must never mean that we lose faith in healing. But healing cannot properly start until some acceptance of the imbalance and its process has been attained. Complete healing can only take place when the nature of our imbalance or illness has been understood. Imbalance and disease carry a wisdom and guidance within them. In order to receive this wisdom and unlock the full power of the body to heal itself, we need to explore the symbolic nature of our ills.

UNDERSTANDING THE WISDOM WITHIN IMBALANCE AND DIS-EASE

Finding the wisdom within dis-ease or imbalance involves interpreting symptoms as symbols. Our bodies speak a very simple, even primitive, language. Attunement to the root chakra enables us to be more in touch with our bodies and the language they speak. We get most from symbols when we seek to live alongside them for a while, rather than rushing to interpret them intellectually. Symbols are rich and many-faceted, yet in another sense economical, since out of apparent simplicity comes so much. Recognizing that a symbol exists starts a communication process with it, and within ourselves.

When we experience difficulties and oppositions which we cannot immediately deal with, or choose to ignore, our bodies tend to produce symptoms. In areas where we have been heavily conditioned by parents or society to live a certain lifestyle or achieve certain standards, the mind tries to exert willpower over emotion and even over matter. Our emotions help us to question the old order and encourage us to find and live our own personal truths and values. The body interacts and colludes with the emotions. Eventually, if the bodily symptoms are pressing enough, we *have* to change our lifestyle, even if only to take a few days' sick leave.

The body does not become ill without reason. Some bodily weak spots may be karmic and need to be interpreted mainly in the light of what has gone before in this chapter. Most of us have constitutionally vulnerable areas and, when we are stressed by life or relationships, tend to produce a certain type of symptom. An initial look at the language of the symptoms may help us to understand the symbolic message they are giving.

My back and neck are my most vulnerable areas. When I get neck pain I have learned to ask the following questions:

- Am I being stiff-necked about something?
- Could I gain from being *more* stiff-necked about something?
- Is something (or someone!) being a 'pain in the neck' to me?
- Am I being a 'pain in the neck' to myself or someone else?

   – Am I 'sticking my neck out' unnecessarily about some
    matter?
   – Ought I to 'stick my neck out' more in the present situation?

Each question must always be reversed – and in the end I am
the only one who can answer it!

   Similarly, with my back, I need to ask:

– Am I being too rigid?
– Am I being too flexible?
– Is someone 'on my back'?
– Am I on someone else's back?
– Am I carrying too much, for myself or others?
– Am I carrying enough? Taking enough responsibility?

Recently I caught a virus, which left my body, particularly my
legs, full of aches and pains. I lost any ease of movement and
had to do everything much more slowly. I had known for some
time that I was living at a very hectic pace and sometimes
forcing myself to keep it up. My body was asking me to slow
down. I interpreted this as quite a serious warning and have
since tried to rest more, to look after my body, to take some
more space for myself and to get some of my commitments
into proportion.

   The symbolic language of symptoms helps us to begin our
understanding of bodily messages but, at a deeper level, it can
also lead us to explore bodily *memory* and its links with our
emotions.

   The following case illustrates and amplifies some of these
issues.

Case Study: Bodily Memory

Chloe, a West Indian client, whose family came to live in
Southern England before she was one year old, wanted to
explore the symbolism of a pulled ankle tendon.

   The original injury had occurred two years previously

whilst she and her partner were leading a group into a dance at a social gathering. The continuing pain, stiffness and weakness in her ankle were still resistant to improvement. She had explored the possibilities that she was carrying too much on behalf of others, or not being true to herself (following her own path). These were true insights and she had taken steps to redress some balances, yet her ankle still did not heal. Medical investigation simply confirmed that the tendons had been sprained and were still weak. There was no other physical injury or contributory cause.

Chloe's *right* ankle was affected. The right side of the body is symbolically associated with the aspects of life which demand focus, direction, thrust, active masculine principle (yang), energy. The left side connects with the areas of life which need diffuse awareness, subtlety, yielding, receptive, receding, feminine principle (yin) energy.

Bearing this in mind, I asked Chloe whether she most often put her right, masculine, yang, leadership side forward in life, or whether she tended to function more from her feminine, yielding, receptive side?

Chloe felt that life itself had pushed her towards being 'up front', 'in the lead' and 'visible'. She was an attractive woman, in a good partnership, but felt that in many ways the development of her truly feminine side had taken a back seat. Her family had always pushed her to do well at school. In art classes she had discovered a talent for design but had never been allowed to enjoy it in a relaxed way. Any gift had to be seriously fostered, and she had been expected to work hard, get top grades and go on to get a degree. She thoroughly enjoyed her present job, working with a design and display team for a large organization, yet she often had a sense of frustration and felt that her talent had always been too developed and focused. She had never been able to enjoy it for its own sake or to 'dabble' with all the potentials which might have been open to her.

Remarking that the injury to her ankle had occurred when

she was leading others into a dance, I asked her to consider whether her right ankle might be telling her that the masculine side needed a rest, and that it could be time to give the left, feminine, side more chance to develop. She felt that this explanation was too simplistic and that there was something deeper and more complex involved.

I asked Chloe to close her eyes and see what image came to mind when she considered her right ankle and its injury. After a while she said she could see herself, aged about seven years old, in a Brownie uniform. The word 'tenderfoot' accompanied this image.

I asked Chloe to associate to the word and the image and she began to talk about a phase in her life which had never clearly come into her memory before.

As a tenderfoot Brownie, working towards full enrolment, which would mean receiving her Brownie badge, and becoming a full Brownie member, Chloe was required to do at least one good turn every day. In order to keep a check on this, and literally, to gain 'Brownie points', Brown Owl had given each of the tenderfoot Brownies a card and some 'stick-on' stars. As good turns were done, so a star could be stuck onto the card. At the end of each week, before the Brownie meeting, Chloe had to get one of her parents to sign the card and verify the number of good turns completed that week.

Chloe's parents had required her, from a very young age, to share tasks in the household. They told her that any good turn for her Brownie membership had to be something over and above the things she was normally expected to do. Since, as a seven-year-old, quite a lot was already demanded of her, she had difficulty in finding something extra each day which her parents would agree to mark on her card as her good turn. Indeed, if she had not done one of her usual chores to perfection even the extra 'good turn' was not considered worthy of a star. At the next Brownie meeting Chloe had the least number of good turns on her record. She knew that her friends did not help in the home nearly as much as she did and was desperately upset when the Brown Owl told her that she obviously needed to try harder if she truly wanted to be an enrolled Brownie. She was unable to explain to her parents what was happening. They consistently refused to consider anything which was within their normal high demands on her as a good turn. Eventually, in desperation and though it cut her off from many of her friends, Chloe gave up Brownies and the tenderfoot requirements. She was then criticized by her parents for lack of commitment.

As this memory surfaced, Chloe realized that there were similar factors operating in her current situation. Although she loved her work, knew she was good at it and often willingly worked unpaid overtime, she was continually being overlooked or under-rewarded when it came to promotions and salary rises. She recognized that she tended not to fight this particular corner. Although, as a black woman in a white culture, she had learned the value of self-assertion, she now saw that she did not expect to be paid or rewarded for her dedication. She felt she had to be more than exceptional before recognition could come her way. She was doing more than others in the team but not getting her 'brownie points'.

In relation to her foot, Chloe now realized that she was often putting her 'best foot forward' to the point of stress and without receiving her just reward or support. Her physical foot had been showing her that something was lacking and that an old pattern needed to be recognized and dealt with. She needed more balance between right and left, yin and yang, and also to make sure she used her yang side to see that she was fairly treated. An underlying resentment was beginning to surface which might affect her decisions about, and attitudes to, her work.

A few weeks later she reported that she had requested, and been awarded, a long overdue promotion and pay award. Her right foot was much less painful and she felt that it was healing successfully at last. We had got to the root cause of the continuing tender foot.

THE DIMENSION ADDED BY THE CROWN CHAKRA

When seeking this kind of insight, working with the root chakra, (as suggested on pages 41–45 and in Exercise 3, page 35) helps the body and the unconscious mind to explore symptoms and symbols more deeply. The dimension added by the crown chakra is that when we stimulate and feed it, as suggested on pages 41–45, a wider facility for understanding our life lessons will be activated.

Chloe was interested in knowing more about her spiritual path, and had been working with her chakras in order to access extra dimensions of information about her ankle. As her ankle healed she became aware that all her life she had been pushed to excel and to have high standards in worldly and mundane spheres. She surmised that she must be balancing a lifetime in which another personality bead had perhaps been lax and uncaring about these, or other areas. She also understood that high standards and self-discipline could be very positive tools to help her live efficiently in the world and learned to let spiritual meaning blend with, and enhance, the task of living to the full. Chloe felt a deeper connection with her higher self and its intentions in choosing her parents, early environment and even her colour, as she got a clearer insight into, and acceptance of, these aspects of her life task.

Case studies are chosen because they are as close as possible to 'textbook' illustrations of points under discussion. You may find that, for you, the issues are not always as clear as mine or Chloe's in their final revelation. Sometimes it is necessary to persevere and wait for insight, but refusing to accept that we are all subject to 'accidents of birth' will help you to open up to fuller self-knowledge at the psychological *and* spiritual levels.

ARCHETYPE: HEALING

Healing should not be seen only in terms of the physical body or the removal of symptoms. It can be described as an archetype since most of us have a drive to perfection or wholeness of body, mind or spirit. As we become conscious of ourselves as individuals and also as part of the human race, we realize that one of our greatest needs is healing. We are all wounded in some aspect of our beings or experience dis-ease within our lives.

Over recent decades we have seen the personal growth movement emerge and flourish. Healing and growth can be synonymous. Gildas has told us not to see healing as an attempt to return to a previously known standard of health but as helping us move on to a new and positive level of health not previously experienced. This enhancement of our health will not occur if healing is merely directed to the removal of symptoms. As we have seen, particularly in the case history of Chloe (see page 58), understanding the language of symptoms leads us to causes of continuing pain or dis-ease which go far deeper than the physical. The body is our evidence for many levels of emotional and spiritual investigation and understanding.

When healing concentrates only on symptoms, or at best, purely physical causes, disease may become chronic or one ailment may be 'cured' only to give way to another. Before true healing can take place, there are messages to comprehend which speak also from the soul. Assimilating these is vital. When we appreciate this, then physical healing as a totality becomes less important. We learn that a state of true health emanates from within our beings and, though we may become physically 'sick unto death', our incarnate spirit can attain a wholeness, or degree of perfection, which shines through and brings blessing and inspiration to others.

Seeing health or beauty as totally body-orientated is narcissistic. To be stuck in narcissism is to remain ignorant both of the greater depths and purposes which life can reveal and of the complex interactions of body, mind, spirit and emotions. Healing is balance and balance is healing.

Of course healing should concern itself with the relief of distressing symptoms and the trials of pain. Yet removing a headache, without addressing the stress which caused it, might eventually lead to physical breakdown. Minor symptoms are an early warning system and should never be ignored or masked by taking a medicament – whether it be from the allopathic *or* complementary range. Healing into ourselves is attained when there is alignment between crown and root chakras and when we take the serious steps towards true self-expression which this alignment may demand. Spirit and soul speak through our emotions. When we neglect the emotions they speak through our bodies; and our bodies give us evidence of our karma and spiritual tasks. The revelation of these will enable true purpose to be released and deep healing to take place. When we widen our paradigms so that it is the essence of a person, not the physical vehicle, which determines our standards, even the most 'imperfect' body, with the spirit shining through, becomes beautiful.

Death itself can be seen as a healing when we consider a greater life cycle than the relatively brief span of one earth life. It is not futile to hope for eventual total healing for all if we believe in the immortality of the life-spark and the eternity of being. Healing, as a process of entering a previously unknown state of health, then becomes synchronous with spiritual evolution.

EXERCISES

The more direct work with crown and root chakras and their colours and archetypes given in Chapters 1 and 2 forms a background to the exercises given here. The more your crown and root chakras are in alignment, the more the information you are seeking will be assisted into your consciousness.

As you have been reading this chapter, you have probably begun to reflect on your own body: its weaknesses, strengths, symptoms and symbols. This exercise is designed to take you, step by step, through the exploration of symptom as symbol. It can be helpful to share an exercise such as this with a partner, or with a group of friends. Suggestions from others and pooling of resources for interpreting symbolism can be very helpful. If you decide to do this, or to discuss your own material with a friend, it is important to remember that:

– There are no categorical meanings.
– There are no quickly accessible 'neat' solutions.
– One person's view, insight or intuition should always be offered as a suggestion and never forced on to the one who is exploring symptoms or symbols. It is essential that the 'protagonist' should come to their own acceptable insights at their own pace and in their own time.
– Unconscious and newly surfacing material is sometimes highly defended. Unless it is very gently encouraged, or given 'permission' to emerge with patience and support, the defences may grow stronger rather than opening up.
– Battering away too strongly at your own or another's defence system may amount to self-abuse or 'psychological rape'.
– When the psyche is unhurried, with its insights gently sought and respected, it will give of its wisdom.
– Symbols which have many layers to be understood are the language and wisdom of the psyche (see Glossary).

Exercise 9
Symptom as Symbol

Before you begin this exercise, know which bodily symptom you wish to explore. Only attempt to explore one symptom at a time. You can repeat the exercise for other symptoms, or to gain a deeper insight into the same symptom, at frequent, regular, or irregular intervals. (I would suggest that 'frequent' is no more than twice a week.)

Have crayons, paper and writing materials to hand.

The exercise is in three parts. *Leave at least two days between each part.*

Part 1: Some Important Questions and Reflections

Making sure that you will be undisturbed, sit or lie comfortably so that your body is symmetrically arranged and can relax. Be in touch with the rhythm of your breathing and practise the 'central column breathing', running from crown to root and root to crown (see page 17). Gradually let your breath rhythm return to normal.

- Focus your attention on the area, organ or function of your body affected by the symptom. Internally ponder the following questions:
  a) What is the name of this area, organ or function of your body?
  b) Do you, or your family have a 'pet name' or non-anatomical name for this area, organ or function?
  c) What is the natural function of this organ or area of your body?
  d) How is that natural function being inhibited at present?
  e) Is the symptom affecting your right or left side?
  f) How do you, or would you, describe your symptom/disease to another person?
  g) If you have pain, what are the words you would use to describe it?
  For (f) and (g) above, give your imagination full rein. See whether there are emotive words which come naturally, e.g. 'I feel as if I am on the rack'; 'I am being dragged down'; 'I am being stabbed'; 'It is a shooting pain'; 'I feel sick [nauseous, want to vomit, sick at heart]'; 'It grips me like a vice'; 'It takes all my energy away'; 'It diminishes

me'; 'It makes me helpless [dependent, despairing]'; 'It gets me down'. There are any number of possibilities. The words which come most naturally to you could be full of symbolic meaning.

- Now write down all your thoughts. Reflect on the symbolic content of what you have written and felt. Ponder the symbolic function of the affected area of your body or bodily function. Consider the symbolic significance of any pet or family names you use for the affected area or function. As you contemplate the significance of left- and right-sided symptoms look again at page 59.
- Now ask yourself: 'Are there situations or people in your life which could be described similarly to the way in which you describe your symptom or pain?'
- Begin to consider ways in which you could help yourself:
  - Do you need some kind of break?
  - Do you need to ask for more help and support in your life, or with your work?
  - Are you nurturing yourself sufficiently?
  - Are you being too receptive or passive? Do you need to change or modify this?
  - Are you being too assertive or aggressive? Do you need to change or modify this?
  - Are you turning anger inwards? Could you express it differently or explore its origins more?
  - Do you need to consider or set in motion a significant life change?
  - Do you need to meditate on 'acceptance'? (see page 56)

Remember that you can separate the parts of this exercise by days or weeks but leave at least two days before attempting Part 2. Do not attempt too much insight too soon or be tempted to try to force or create a flood of insights.

The psyche (see Glossary) has its own wisdom and timing. It responds best when you respect these and gently encourage its revelations. Hidden or symbolic meanings and unsuspected inner dynamics have usually developed as survival mechanisms or valuable defences when life was threatening. If you approach with care and respect for yourself and your inner processes, the defences will gradually melt and allow you access to the treasures of insight. If, as you meet obstacles within yourself, you try to tear them down or blow them apart they will tend to get stronger, for they are like scar tissue round a wound.

A gentle approach allows the scar tissue to soften so that deep healing can happen and the nature of the wound be fully known. Impatience creates new scarring, underneath which the wound may continue to suppurate. Remember that visualizations often present you with well-known material, which the psyche, in its wisdom, may be asking you to look at from a new angle. When you are ready to hear your own story, with wonder, empathy and without judgement, it will unfold, episode by episode.

A client of mine who was very impatient and judgemental with herself longed for her inner journeys and visualizations to be rich and revelatory. Even when they were, she had difficulty acknowledging their significance – she was always pushing for more. Gradually she realized that she must first learn to be a less stern self-critic in order to hear and see herself more clearly. She worked to become less of a perfectionist in her expectations and eventually had a beautiful dream in which a forest which had been totally ravaged by fire was to be carefully excavated by experts who had the secret of nurturing new growth. This dream presaged the release of her long-blocked creativity and the relaxing of her deep defences.

If you are ever in doubt about self-exploration it is wise to seek advice from a counsellor or therapist. Transpersonally trained counsellors and therapists will usually be most helpful with visualization techniques (see Glossary).

Part 2 Image or Symbol

You will need crayons or pastels and paper for this second part of the exercise.

Make the same initial preparations as for Part 1. Practise central column breathing (see page 17). Then let your breathing find its normal rhythm.

- With your eyes closed, and with the same symptom in mind that you used for Part 1 of this exercise, imagine that you are looking at an inner screen. Mentally ask for a symbol, or an image representing your symptom, to appear on your screen.
- After five minutes, take your paper and colours and draw this image meditatively, letting it develop more fully as you draw. Take as long as you need to complete the drawing to your satisfaction.
- Even if no image or symbol appeared on your inner screen, try to let something emerge freely on paper as you doodle or draw. Do not be concerned about your drawing ability or the quality of your drawing. You are seeking to bring information from the inner world to the outer and drawing is one of the ways in which this can be accomplished. Only if you are really inhibited about drawing should you use words as a description instead.

Wait at least two days before attempting Part 3 of this exercise. In the intervening time look often at your drawing without trying to interpret the image or symbol intellectually.

Part 3 Bodily Memory

Making sure that you will be undisturbed, read over the notes you made for Part 1 of this exercise and consider again your drawing of your image or symbol from Part 2.

Sitting, or lying down, practise central column breathing (see page 17). Gradually let your breathing return to its normal rhythm.

- Using the same symptom as for Parts 1 and 2 of this exercise, focus your attention on the relevant part of your body or bodily function. Look back over your life, mentally asking your memory to bring to mind anything which could be associated with the symptoms you are now experiencing. Do not judge or criticize what your memory finds. At this point it is particularly important not to examine the relevance of what your psyche is offering you. Do not strive to get memories from childhood. Something which happened to you more recently could be significant in opening up further or deeper insights. When you feel ready to do so, write up, as fully as possible, the memory which is coming most insistently to the surface.
- When you have finished writing, read again the passage from Chloe's case study relating to her Brownie tenderfoot (page 60).
- Only now, begin to muse upon what the memory your psyche has given you could mean in relationship to the symbolism of your symptom. Do not reflect too intently. Let the memory remain with you over a period of time and read your write-up of it once a day. Gradually the key words and insights will emerge. They may easily vanish if you do not record them, so write things down immediately as they surface.

Exercise 10
Guided Journey to the Healing Archetype

It can be helpful to speak the words of an inner journey, with appropriate periods of silence, onto a cassette, so that you can listen as you go, rather than trying to remember or follow the instructions from merely reading them through.

If you are unfamiliar with inner journeying you may want to refer to the 'Inner Journeying' entry in the Glossary or one of my previous books, such as *The River of Life* (see Bibliography), before embarking on this exercise.

Making sure that you will be undisturbed and with colours and writing materials to hand, sit or lie in a relaxed position, where your spine can be straight and supported, if necessary, in comfort. Your head should be well-balanced on your neck. Do not cross your legs at the knees or ankles, though a cross-legged or lotus position is favourable, if comfortable for you.

Practise central column breathing (see page 17) until you feel the two-way flow between your crown and root chakras, then gradually let your breathing find its normal rhythm.

- When you are ready, move into your inner space or landscape and find yourself in a meadow. (This may be modelled on an outer meadow you know or remember, or be a meadow which purely exists within.)
- Take the opportunity of being in the meadow to activate all your inner senses . . . See the colours and the objects . . . Hear the sounds . . . Smell the fragrances . . . Touch the textures . . . Taste the tastes . . .
- Beyond the meadow there is undulating countryside leading into steeper hills and mountains . . . As you look out over the landscape, a part of you knows where you need to go in order to meet the archetype of healing . . . (You may travel to water; to a cave; to a hill or mountain top; into a special valley; to a special tree; to a sanctuary;

to a place where there is fire. There are many possibilities which your psyche can open up for you.)

- Once you know in which direction you need to travel you may wish to take companions with you. You can invite your inner wise presence (which may be personified, or could be a light, colour or essence), and a power animal to go with you. Your inner power animals are protectors, guardians and guides. They may be very fierce in the outer wild state, but in your inner world they are your friends and you can communicate with them. You may also wish to take a talisman or amulet (a special object which helps you to centre and be empowered – see Glossary).

- When you are totally ready, begin your journey to the place where you know you will be able to meet your archetype of healing . . . (Five minutes silence.)

- When you arrive at the right place, if your archetype is not immediately there to meet you, look around and explore the area a little and then settle yourself comfortably with your wise presence and your power animal near you and invite your archetype of healing to appear . . . (Two minutes of silence.)

- Greet your archetype of healing . . . Ask if you might be shown a healing sanctuary or temple of colour healing to which you can go now, or on any other occasion when you are in need of healing . . . Your healing archetype will accompany you to this place and see that you receive healing and refreshment . . . (Ten minutes of silence.)

- Before you leave the healing temple or sanctuary and your archetype of healing, ask whether there is any message or symbolic gift to help forward your inner and outer processes of healing and growth . . . Thank your healing archetype and prepare for the journey back to the meadow . . .

- Your healing archetype may accompany you back to your meadow, or may stay in the area around the sanctuary or temple . . . Certainly your inner wise presence and your

power animal will travel back with you . . . Make the
journey in your own time . . . and then move from the
meadow to an awareness of the rhythm of your
breathing . . . Be aware of your body on the floor, couch or
chair . . . Breathe the central column breath . . . Imagine
that you are surrounded by a cloak of light with a hood,
and then return fully to your outer surroundings to
draw and record your journey.

Exercise 11
Considering Gender

Gender and its inevitable outcome of sexuality are major
themes in our lives. This exercise is based on the introductory
questions on page 48. Another exercise relating to issues of
sexuality is Exercise 23, page 150.

Making sure that you will be undisturbed and that you have
pen or pencil, coloured crayons and paper to hand, read
again the section on gender on page 49.

- Now practise central column breathing until you feel
  centred and relaxed. Take a sheet of paper and, if you are
  female, write the heading: 'I am a woman'. If you are male
  write the heading 'I am a man'. Use colour for the heading
  if you wish.
- Reflect on this heading for a few moments and then write
  the sub-heading: 'This means that: . . .'
- Now take twenty minutes to half an hour, to reflect on what
  your gender means to you, how you feel about it and the
  messages which society gives about it. As you write your lists
  and comments be aware of any tensions in your body and
  the areas in which you are holding them. Do not analyse
  what you have written too strongly at this moment; just
  let what has come rest in your consciousness. When you
  feel ready to do so, it could be helpful to share your

reflections and comments with a friend or partner if that is possible.

THE COLOURS

The colours for the root chakra are red, brown and mauve; and, for the crown chakra, violet, white and gold. To strengthen the colours in your crown and root chakras refer to Exercise 8 (page 42).

THE FRAGRANCES

For the root chakra the quietening fragrances are cedarwood and patchouli, and the stimulating ones are musk, lavender and hyacinth. For the crown chakra the quietening fragrances are rosemary and bergamot, and the stimulating ones are violet and amber. Refer to page 43 for notes on the use of the fragrances for these chakras.

THE CRYSTALS

Refer to page 44 and the Glossary for general guidance on using crystals. The crystals which will best help the issues considered in this chapter are:

White Tourmaline To encourage integrity and facilitate the deeper understanding of spiritual surrender and obedience. This is a spiritually purifying stone which promotes inner honesty and insight.

Smoky Quartz To promote calmness, centring and grounding. It helps to calm fear and panic and minimizes shock.

Garnet This crystal aids tissue healing and regeneration and so speeds the healing of actual physical wounds to the body, including those made through surgery. It also brings comfort for loss or bereavement and during all times of life change.

PRAYERS OF AFFIRMATIONS

The root chakra prayer or affirmation is:

> Through incarnation may spirit be brought into matter.
> Through rootedness may life-force be recharged and exchanged. We acknowledge wholeness and seek to gain and to reflect acceptance.

The crown chakra prayer or affirmation is:

> Through surrender and release let the incoming will be truly the will of God working within us and through us, leading us increasingly to knowledge of mystical union and mystical marriage.

For suggestions on using the prayers or affirmations, see page 45.

Chapter 4

The Tentacles of the Octopus:
Improving Family Relationships

Key Issues: Healing the Family of Origin, Improving Family
Relationships, the Inner Child
Chakra Triad: Root, Heart and Crown
Archetypes: Great Mother and Great Father

This chapter will help you gain:
- insight into the karmic reasons for your choice of parents
- information about spiritual and genetic families
- an understanding of the needs of the inner child
- knowledge of how to heal family pains and wounds
- insight into what may go wrong in relationships with friends,
  colleagues and lovers

AREAS OF INFLUENCE

For lists of the areas of influence of the root and crown chakras
see pages 19–21.

The Heart Chakra:

Location On the same level as the physical heart, but in the centre of the body (stem at back).

Key Words Compassion, Feeling, Tenderness, Love of God, Love of Others, Detachment

Developmental Age 12–15 years

Colours Spring Green, Rose, Rose Amethyst

Element Air

Sense Touch

Body Feeling

Glandular Connection Thymus

Quietening Fragrances Sandalwood, Rose

Stimulating Fragrances Pine, Honeysuckle

Crystals and Gemstones Emerald, Green Calcite, Amber, Azurite, Chrysoberyl, Jade, Rose, Watermelon Tourmaline

Prayer or Affirmation

In the golden centre of the rose of the heart may tender compassion be linked to unconditional love. May true detachment enable growth and continuity. Through the understanding of birth within death and death within birth may there be transformation.

THE HEART CHAKRA AND LIFE

When the heart chakra is healthy and flexible the link between the concerns of root and crown becomes alive and less clinical or esoteric. The sense for the heart chakra is that of touch. As we come into incarnation we touch the earth and are touched by it physically, emotionally and symbolically. A native American Indian saying states that nothing exists except in relationship to something else. Thus, through touch we form relationships and create our existence.

The science of human behaviour has clearly established that

living creatures need to be touched in order to thrive. Yet European cultures, in particular, often have difficulties with touch. A tendency to want to be told how to, rather than relying on our instincts, about the bearing and nurturing of our babies and children, leads to confusion. So-called child experts have, in the past, advised over-strict routines. Before the definitive scientific experiments with touch, almost a whole generation of babies was deprived of natural fondling and caressing on the advice of Truby King, an influential American paediatrician.

Left untouched in their cots for the recommended four hours between feeds, crying babies could be checked for wind or protruding nappy pins but were trained to express hunger only by the clock. The thought that small babies might need loving touch, comfort and stimulation, as well as warmth and food, was denied. Mothers who obeyed their instincts and enjoyed interim cuddles with their babies were told that they were being 'conditioned' by the child and storing up discipline problems for later. A generation of touch-deprived babies, and of parents denied a natural instinctive pleasure in their children, makes a big impact on society, dampening qualities of the heart and suppressing creativity.

The connection of the heart chakra to the sense of touch, gives us the central issue for heart chakra functioning. The word 'touch' must be understood in its full meaning. We touch each other physically but we are also touched by each other emotionally. The symbolism of touch comes into our language when we use such phrases as 'keep in touch' or 'I'll be in touch'.

The other heart chakra key words arise mainly from the wider meanings and applications of touch. These are: compassion, feeling, tenderness, love of God, and love of others. In considering these key words, and what they may say to you about the condition of your own heart chakra, it is essential to ask yourself whether you are able to *receive* these qualities from others as well as *give* them. Perhaps most difficult of all, you should also consider whether you have a healthy love for yourself as well as for others.

The key word of 'detachment' may seem a strange one to apply to the heart chakra, yet it is crucial in enabling us to differentiate between basic emotion and the true feeling quality of the heart. Traditionally the symbol of the heart, as seen on Valentine's Day cards, is associated with emotion and romantic love; it is also considerably overworked in terms of love of places, food, or makes of car.

True heart love is constant, warm and goes beyond the fires of passion. Of course we need romance and burning ardour, but in true chakra terms these belong more to the sacral and solar plexus than to the heart (see page 132). The heart *chakra* is not the seat of the emotions but of feeling. The subtle body connection for the heart is the 'feeling body'. When the heart chakra unfolds there is a progression from the gut-level emotions of the sacral centre, through self-awareness at the solar plexus, to a shining quality of feeling, tempered with wisdom.

The truly heart-centred individual brings a feeling quality to life without being governed by raw emotion. It is possible to have, acknowledge and use feeling without it controlling our lives in a way which evades rationality and responsibility. These emotions can be harnessed without being denied. Their energies can be used advisedly, enhancing empowerment of self and others. Thus, *detachment* does not mean cold or uncaring withdrawal but the discipline which enables us to see an emotive situation with clarity and make a dispassionate appraisal of problems in order to act with the love which is both enhanced and tempered by wisdom. Understood in this way, detachment can be the midwife who brings love and wisdom to birth.

As you look into your own heart chakra, a question to ask is: 'How do I touch the world and how does the world touch me?' If, as is likely, your considered responses to this question indicate blockages, then working with the root/heart/crown chakra combination will be of particular value.

ROOT, HEART AND CROWN AS A CHAKRA TRIAD

Chapters 2 and 3 examined the relationship and interactions between the root and crown chakras, emphasizing the part they play in helping us to understand our major incarnational choices as well as the way in which our selection of physical body and constitution is related to issues of purpose and evolution.

The heart enables relationship. The interaction of crown and root in manifesting the purposes of the higher self can seem cold, clinical or even calculating without the heart element. Less the qualities of heart, the whole plan of incarnation and evolution on earth could be seen as something of a life sentence – to be endured until we can return to softer realms.

Because the heart chakra plays a major part in enabling us to feel love, it also puts us in touch with our pain. As human beings, we know and identify our feelings by contrast or because of polarities. In experiencing the lighter side of life and tender feelings, such as love, joy, fulfilment, security and passion, we also open ourselves to the *heartache* conditions of loneliness, lack of love, sadness, frustration, insecurity and boredom. Often it is the negative experience which spurs us on to transformation, to seek higher ideals, to serve each other and society and aspire to a higher potential for humankind. In a more perfect society we would hope for love, rather than the lack of it, to be the major catalyst.

The heart chakra gives us a more direct and personal relationship with our tasks. In engendering in us 'a love of God' or, more widely interpreted, a search for positive meaning and pattern, it helps us to place ourselves within the greater plan of the universe and to understand the function of the microcosm. Using Exercise 12 on page 97 will help you to be more in touch with your heart chakra energy and to strengthen the important flow between root, heart and crown chakras.

THE FAMILY OF ORIGIN

In terms of life choices the heart chakra is most linked to family affiliations and the learning and growth which come from them. At soul level, a careful overview is made as to our choice of parents and the experiences which being brought into incarnation and reared by them will give us.

Gildas explains that at the higher levels of our existence we all belong to soul groups or families. He asks us to:

Imagine a tree, then the forest in which it stands, then many other forests of trees. Twigs, leaves, fruits and flowers which spring from the same branch are soul families. Branches on the same tree, or the tree seen as a whole, are soul groups. Forests are wider soul groups. In life you meet those who are from the same branch as yourself and will often recognize them joyfully as your true 'spiritual family'. This means that genetic family is not necessarily spiritual family, and recognition of this can often ease the build-up of expectations within the genetic family.

You will also meet with those who are from your own tree and those who are of your wider group soul. Often so-called 'difficult karma' comes from the efforts of soul family and group to mirror lessons for each other. The impulse of this mirroring comes from love and understanding and will have relevance to the joint evolution of the group.

You are never alone. You always have soul family and soul group contacts around you and joint work to be recognized and carried out. Sometimes you may seem to be living in conditions of isolation, or in alien territory. Even when the direct contacts are not there, try to sense all the subtle energetic forces of love and acceptance surrounding you.

Choice of Parents

Our acceptance and comprehension of our choice of parents and families will depend initially on the nature of our encounter with them. If our parents have been welcoming, loving, supportive, communicative, united, understanding, generous and just, then putting down roots, finding our true identity and being content to be human can be a natural, joyful progression. Our entry into incarnation is eased, allowing the heart chakra to open naturally and function strongly.

It is, however, in the nature of parents to be less than perfect. Psychologically it has been suggested that they can, at best, be only 'good enough'. It may be problematic for us to accept that we have 'chosen' parents who have been less than welcoming, loving and supportive, and the thought of choosing a hostile or even rejecting early environment may be incomprehensible. Our reactions to our initial surroundings affect the relationship between root and crown as well as the development of a fully functioning heart chakra.

The physical family of origin into which we incarnate will reflect and be the means of implementing some of the purposes of soul family evolution. As part of this implementation we may either choose to be born into a family where we know and subtly recognize our parents and siblings or into a family which has been chosen for other reasons, such as genetic, cultural or social inheritance. It is also possible that the choice of family may be connected to the balancing and reparation of direct karma, providing an opportunity to meet our most challenging lessons and teachers.

When we are among those we love and remember, making the transition from the other worlds to the material plane is very easy, and the problems of rooting, grounding and being incarnate are lessened. This option may be taken perhaps as a contrast to a previous lonely or traumatic incarnation, or when our main incarnational focus is the development of a special gift. In such a case we may choose to incarnate to those who will nurture us in every way and protect us from having to give energy to the overcoming of serious life obstacles.

When we select a more hostile or difficult early environment, with parents and siblings who are not of our soul wavelength or group, then much of our learning will be centred around the obstacles we encounter and the consciousness dealing with these will engender. Some difficulties are chosen in order to help us understand the effects of causes we set in motion in another lifetime, others simply to provide a challenge and hone our strengths. Having to fight for one's identity is not easy, but it leads towards greater self-knowledge and self-appreciation of a healthy kind.

Dodi Smith wrote a well-known play, entitled *Dear Octopus*, about the family, its powers, strengths, influences and weaknesses. The octopus is known, and feared, for its ability to stretch out its long tentacles, grip hard and squeeze the life-force from its victim. It also squirts a dark ink, when being pursued, in order to confuse its predators. According to myth, if one tentacle of the octopus is cut off, another will immediately grow. It can be a hero's task to escape its grip and slay the life-threatening monster. The last line of Dodi Smith's play is: 'Whose tentacles we never quite forget'.

Even in the most positive sense, families make demands and their influence shapes our lives. We all need to 'belong' and this need gives great power to families of all kinds. Family strength and sustenance may be our mainstay; unconditional family love our solace. Pride in our kith and kin can be an inspiration. Genetically, we carry the family within us and our genealogical heredity forms an important part of our identity. When loyalties are under duress the well-known saying 'blood is thicker than water' is often proved true.

Conversely, family commitments may be limitations. Issues

of personal freedom and the process of finding our true selves can be aided or impeded by family dynamics. Grandparents, parents and siblings are strong forces, affecting the psychological formation of the individual psyche. Negative family currents, such as jealousies, enmities and the negative power of possessive love, may seem to sap our spirit. The themes of the perils of divided loyalties, rigid expectations and lack of permission are constantly reflected back to us by writers of potent novels and dramas. Yet psychological struggles, vitality-sapping as they may be, have a wider scale of reference when given a spiritual dimension and seen against the continuum of more than one lifetime. The concept of the evolution of the soul can inspire us through the bitterest struggles and ensure that we do not fall victim to a sense of meaninglessness.

Karmically, the family is our nurturer, teacher and the back-drop against which we learn about life. The greater families of society, nation or race also influence and condition us power-fully. The expectations of our society affect those of our family of origin. Certain moral and ethical requirements and con-formities are part of the search for justice and help to oil the wheels of life. Within the different strata of society, there are social mores, fashions, and power games which influence fam-ilies and their vision. Parents largely condition children to conform to the models that society or a particular culture find acceptable or desirable at any given time. When individuals are seen as clay to be moulded or forced into a convenient shape, rather than seeds with an inbuilt potential to blossom, the negative pressures of family dynamics can seriously affect the individual search for identity and self-worth.

At the more subtle level of the spiritual family or soul group, our inbuilt potential is fully known. Yet, even here, the con-ditions of our incarnation will be affected by the need to work not only for our own evolution but also for that of the group. Evolution is something which the individual achieves as part of a soul family and aspects of the 'brief' we bring with us into incarnation will go beyond our personal needs to reflect the higher-level family task.

The process of incarnation, being present on earth, and being born into a specific family of origin, in order to further our personal evolution as well as that of our soul family and group is thus immensely complex. Gildas tells us that, from the level of the higher selves of the soul family group, we contemplate the interweaving threads of incarnations as might a group of actors standing in the wings of a stage and planning the moves for the enactment of a drama. Those who, on earth, seem to be our harshest taskmasters, may be very close to us in our soul group. When there is an important lesson to be learned, we play confrontational roles for each other if this will enable the learning to take place sooner rather than later. It can take deep love to face the pain of being the catalyst for another's learning if any degree of suffering is involved.

Our evolutionary learning, derived from many lifetimes, is recorded and stored within our chakras. As more experience is recorded, so the chakras themselves mature and evolve. Family dynamics, from the soul level, through the total family of humanity, to our immediate incarnate family of origin, are intricately connected to the heart chakra. The developed heart chakra causes us to turn living into an art. It demands that we relate to the wider, as well as the immediate family, as part of our search for meaning and purpose in life. The heart chakra is unfolding and engaging when we feel that it is no longer enough to accept the conditions of life on earth as unalterable or merely to identify a task and get on with it.

The interaction between root, heart and crown chakras leads to a more passionate reality. Families form the arena within which our feelings are played out. Strong families, where relationship skills are inherent or have been worked for, sustain intensity well and become even stronger when faced with the inevitable challenges and woundings of growth. A self-healing mechanism may seem to operate. Less close-knit families, when under stress, can be so wounded as to become dysfunctional.

A vicious circle of wounding and re-wounding may occur and active healing intervention may be required. The following case study reflects some of these issues.

Case Study: Family Dynamics

Thomas, in his early sixties, married to Joyce, had recently been diagnosed as having Parkinson's disease. Hoping to gain perspective for the current and future challenges of his difficult, degenerative and incurable condition, he had decided to look back over his life. By so doing he had hoped to form a plan for the future and the management of his illness. Instead, what he saw and the value judgments he had brought to his review had made him extremely depressed. Joyce had recently read one of my books and managed to persuade Thomas to book a personal appointment. They came to talk to me together.

He told me that he felt a failure, and could see little meaning or purpose either in his own life or in life as a whole. He came from what he described as 'humble origins'. His father had been a farm labourer but had voluntarily 'joined up' as soon as the war began. He was killed in action whilst Thomas was still a young child. Thomas left school as soon as possible, feeling that he was the man of the house and responsible for helping his mother. He trained in carpentry but as he was becoming established in his work he suffered greatly when his mother, still relatively young, met and married another man. Although they offered him a home he preferred to find lodgings. He harboured a deep resentment towards his mother for having, as he felt, betrayed the memory of his father.

Although Thomas enjoyed carpentry and was good at it, he had artistic skills which did not find expression in the straightforward work he was required to do. He met Joyce, a nurse at the local cottage hospital, when he had to attend for regular dressings on an infected wound originally caused by the slip of a chisel. Though Thomas would occasionally use the lathe to make a beautiful bowl or other wooden objects, he continued as a regular carpenter until retirement.

Joyce gave up nursing when their two children, Frances and Gary, were born with barely eighteen months between them. Thomas loved his children dearly but, as they grew older, determined that they should pursue careers which would give them a different lifestyle to any he had known. His vision for Frances was that she should work in an environment where she might meet a husband who would lift her from the social level in which he felt himself to be stuck. For Gary, his vision was of the banking world, with eventual progression to bank manager.

Joyce confirmed that he had put a lot of pressure on the children as they neared school-leaving age to enter careers that he, rather than they, had chosen. Frances became an air hostess and Gary began his career in banking. Both had indicated that there were other choices they would prefer, since both had inherited their father's latent artistic gifts. Gary had begged to be trained in carpentry and Frances longed for drama school but their objections had been over-ruled.

When Frances saved all her wages from the airline and eventually worked her way through drama school and into repertory work, Thomas had been devastated. When Gary left banking to learn wood-turning he was distraught. His relationship with his children had broken down. Frances's artistic and creatively dressed friends and boyfriends horri-fied him and, as Gary began to be successful in his chosen career, he would hardly speak to him when he came to visit.

Joyce loved Thomas very much, but she too had suffered from his narrow views and frustrations about their social standing in life. She had been very angry when he had thwarted her desire to return to her career. She had resolved her dilemma by taking an interest in counselling and eventually in spiritual subjects. She had pointed out to Thomas that he was jealous of Gary who was doing something which really lay close to Thomas's own heart, and she had supported her daughter in her determination to follow her own way rather than act out her pre-planned destiny. Joyce said that both children understood that their father had always only wanted the best for them but, since they had both made their life changes, they found it difficult to cope with Thomas's open antagonism and barely suppressed rage.

Both Frances and Gary were living with partners, but there were no plans yet, it seemed, for grandchildren. Thomas also had difficulty accepting the trend for living together without marriage. The family dynamic had broken down.

As Thomas reviewed all this, he was full of regrets and frustrations. At first these were directed towards others: he felt that what he saw as his care for others had been rejected. His rage at this was considerable. He accused his children of spoiling his life. As we worked together, though, he gradually began to see that he was also angry and frustrated with himself and there was a big breakthrough point when he felt able to express the distressing but insightful thought that it was perhaps not his children who had spoiled his life, but he who had made big difficulties for Frances and Gary. Gradually he began to admire the spirit and determination they had both shown in finding their own way through life.

Big changes in thinking and expectations, like these, do not come quickly or easily. Whatever insights Thomas had, there was still no cure for his Parkinsonism. Nor could he fulfil his frustrated artistic talent, since the tremor and rigidity of Parkinsons now made working with tools dangerous. Aided and encouraged by Joyce, Thomas did change greatly. Eventually he began to explore the spiritual approach to meaning in life and found solace in the thought that Frances and Gary had chosen himself and Joyce as parents. They had given their children a lot of early love and security, but he could see that maybe they needed to have obstacles in their way to make them more appreciative and conscious about the finding of their true identities. He could also accept that in this present lifetime he had, in himself, to learn about rigidity and to come through it to greater tolerance. He also recognized the rigidity of his concept of masculine and feminine roles. He began to join Joyce in some of her chakra exercises and meditations.

Eventually Thomas's change of heart brought healing to the family dynamic. He became much more tolerant of his children's lifestyles and genuinely interested in their achievements. Joyce still keeps in touch from time to time and in a recent letter told me that Thomas had invested some money, saved over the years, in helping Gary to open his own workshop and small gallery for the production and display of his work. He was able to work in the gallery himself, on a part-time basis, discussing and marketing the lovely objects. Gary often sought his advice about different woods and tools, and father and son had grown much closer. Joyce also told me that Frances was expecting their first grandchild, was shortly to be married and had delighted Thomas by being traditional enough to ask him to 'give her away'.

Had Thomas not come for help and the above story been told by Frances or Gary, there would have been a great deal of emphasis on their frustrations. They might have expressed distress about the role their mother was forced to play. If Thomas had been unable to change, strands of guilt about not fulfilling parental expectations might have affected all their life decisions. If and when they had created their own families the breakdown in communication with their parents could have become more and more painful. The tentacles of the family octopus, so out of touch or cut off in one sense, would have become more complex and powerful.

One of Thomas's greatest original wounds came from the wartime death of his father. As a boy he felt thrust into premature responsibility for his mother. This sense became so strong that, even as a young man, he felt rejected, estranged and undermined when she decided to remarry. A part of him always wanted to regain masculine control, and Joyce and his children suffered because of this. If the eventual family rift had not been healed, the spirit of rebellion could have turned negative in its effect on the future development of Frances and Gary. Frances's decision to have a church wedding and to be 'given away' by her father was a very healing choice. In families, when one healing move or creative compromise is made, others often follow.

The heart chakra, linked to crown and root enables us to relate to the meaning of life. Once meaning dawns, healing, understanding and forgiveness come more easily. Knowing that we are working out an intricate evolutionary plan, as instruments of growth for each other, lifts frustrations and puts anger into perspective. We understand the drama of life as clearly as we might understand a complex play in a theatre.

We need to remember, though, that spiritual, emotional and psychological worlds intermingle just as the spiritual and physical do (see Chapter 3). Finding that detachment from the heart which enables us to take an overview of life's challenges and pains does not of itself heal all the vulnerability within. Frustrations, deprivations, neglect, and the hurt of being unseen and unheard in childhood, go deep. As a preparation for all family healing, the child within must be considered and helped. Without healing, the inner child retains a negative autonomy which often perpetuates a negative influence within the family. As we attempt to make modifications in our lives, all sorts of obstacles may unexpectedly appear. We try to alter the patterns, but they reassert themselves. Usually, at the heart of resistance to change, lies the fear, neediness, uncertainty and suffering of the inner child.

THE INNER CHILD

During childhood it is almost inevitable that parents and teachers will misunderstand or misinterpret our behaviour and needs from time to time. If, for instance, a child is constantly deprived of the right kind of attention, it may discover that being 'naughty' wins notice, and conclude that a negative response, or even punishment, is better than no attention at all. In such a case the true needs of the child are not met. With growth into adulthood, an immature, unsatisfied inner part will live on as a needy and perhaps naughty, neglected and angry inner child. The adult's life and behaviour will be marked, at moments which may come as a surprise or embarrassment, by this autonomous aspect making itself known and felt. (See also Chapter 7, page 165).

The needy aspects of the child within lead us to seek parenting and permission from others, often for much of our lives. We cannot truly empower ourselves to make free choices until we recognize our inner child's needs and take responsibility for healing these parts within ourselves. To make the process more complicated, until we gain fuller insights our own inner censor may reflect our parents' attitudes. Thus we may continue to punish and oppress the fearful, over-indulge the spoiled, and undernourish the hungry children within. Such mechanisms are all part of the complexities of conditioning and can present huge obstacles to family healing unless they are seen as intrinsic to it.

When, as adults, we create our own good inner parent, we take pressure from the family of origin and change the expectations which may still be bound up within it. Self-help for the inner child is very effective. One of the tools for healing is the heart chakra (see Exercise 13, page 98). It should be noted, however, that if the childhood difficulties were severe or overwhelming the help of a trained therapist could be needed.

CUTTING THE TIES THAT BIND

The symbolic image of the octopus is of a creature which holds its victim in a crushing grip which drains life-force away. It binds the victim with its sucker-encrusted tentacles and will not let go. When family relationships become difficult or blocked, before true healing can take place, it may be necessary to cut negative ties. Clairvoyantly, these ties can often be seen as grey pulsating cords which carry a two-way flow of energy, keeping grievances alive, preventing the healing of old patterns and the emergence of the new.

There are ties created by conditioning, emotional blackmail, false or divided loyalties, and unreasonable expectations of, or from, ourselves and others. These affect every aspect of interpersonal and intrapersonal relationships. Once their exist-ence is recognized, their effective cutting or dissolving is aided by visualization and prayer, since, in addition to being psycho-logical mechanisms, they actually exist energetically on the psychic and subtle planes.

You may only have considered ties to be of a valuable and positive nature. The prospect of cutting even those which are subtly destructive can be daunting. Though we crave freedom to be ourselves, we may also fear it. We have negative invest-ments in the things which prevent or hold back our forward progress. Negative patterns have hidden 'benefits' which we should endeavour to understand before attempting to cut the ties and bring ourselves the challenge of freedom.

The ties that bind can give us excuses for not facing the challenges of life. Nelson Mandela reminded us in his famous inaugural speech:

Our deepest fear is not that we are inadequate. Our deepest fear is that we are powerful beyond measure. It is our light, not our darkness, that most frightens us. We ask ourselves, who am I to be brilliant, gorgeous, talented and fabulous? Actually, who are you not to be? You are a child of God – your playing small doesn't serve the world. There is nothing enlightened about shrinking so that other people will not feel insecure around you. We were born to make manifest the glory of God that is within us. It is not in just some of us; it is in everyone. And as we let our own light shine, we unconsciously give people permission to do the same. As we are liberated from our own fear, our presence automatically liberates others.

Positive cutting of the ties that bind means that we release more energy into our lives, cut out negative collusions, provide opportunity for emotional climates to change and leave space for the true, higher nature of our relationships to become clear. True tie-cutting needs the detachment and wisdom of the heart chakra to make it successful. The heart chakra may need negative emotional ties to be cut before it can function at its highest level and help us to stay in positive relationship to others. Far from driving us apart from others, tie-cutting sets us free to love without encumbrance. Two visualizations for tie-cutting, designed by Gildas, are given in Exercise 14 on page 99.

PERSONIFIED ARCHETYPES: THE GREAT MOTHER AND GREAT FATHER

These archetypes have been chosen for this chapter because they lead on from the Sun, Moon and Stars archetypes chosen for Chapter 2 (see page 32). As the heart chakra forms a trio with the root and crown, the qualities of the sun, moon and stars become less remote. The mother/father archetypes can be used for healing the inner child and the family of origin (see Exercise 13, page 98).

An extract from J.C. Cooper, writing of the Great Mother in *An Illustrated Encyclopaedia of Traditional Symbols*, shows

something of the complexity and all-embracing nature of this
archetype:

> She is the archetypal feminine, the origin of all life; the
> containing principle; she symbolizes all phases of cosmic
> life, uniting all the elements, both celestial and chthonic
> [relating to, or inhabiting the underworld]. She is the
> Queen of Heaven, Mother of God, 'opener of the way';
> the keeper of the keys of fertility and the gates of birth,
> death and rebirth. As the Moon Goddess she is perpetual
> renewal, the bringer of the seasons, the controller of the
> life-giving waters. She is the measurer of time, the weaver
> of fate, weaving the web and pattern of life with the
> thread of destiny, symbolic of her power of ensnaring and
> binding, but also of loosing and freeing. She has the dual
> nature of creator and destroyer and is both nourisher,
> protector, provider of warmth and shelter, and the terrible
> forces of dissolution, devouring and death-dealing; she is
> the creator and nourisher of all life and its grave.

The Great Father is also known as the All Father or simply,
The Father. Though also complex, J.C. Cooper's description is
relatively succinct: He is:

> The sun; the Spirit; the masculine principle; conventional
> forces of law and order as opposed to the feminine and
> intuitive instinctual powers. The sky god is the All-Father.
> In myth and legend the figure of the father symbolizes
> physical, mental and spiritual superiority. Father Time,
> identified with Cronos/Saturn, holds a scythe or sickle as
> god of agriculture and as the Reaper, Time. An hourglass
> is also his attribute.

The Great Mother archetype has more negative symbolism
than the Great Father. This is because these archetypes also
largely personify the feminine and masculine principles. The

masculine principle, being more direct, focused and less absorbent, acquires fewer trappings. The feminine principle, in its diffuseness, ability to gestate, give birth and embody the chthonic, encompasses the depths as well as the heights. The Great Mother teaches us more about the shadow side of life than does the Great Father. Yet the Great Father has a major part in creating shadow, since the focused awareness of the masculine principle can lead to a denial of unconscious forces, causing them to gain autonomy.

The Great Mother and Great Father as Healers

In concentrating on the Great Mother and Great Father for individual and family healing, we need to use the highest principles held by these archetypes.

We have expectations of how good mothers and good fathers should be. When our family-of-origin parents are less than exemplary, something within us is dissatisfied. Often long into adult life, even when we have children of our own, an aspect of the inner child may hold the belief that our parents will change overnight and satisfy its outstanding needs. Of course, the adult knows that our parents are as they are. Probably they have done the best they can for us. If they have been totally inadequate, then the adult can see that they were a product of their own environment, and even where conditions have been very traumatic, some compassion may be felt and forgiveness possible. This process of acceptance (see also page 56) is greatly helped by taking a spiritual view of evolution.

The inner child, though, does not accept so easily. Its needs live on, and, for full healing to take place, must be met. If the parents of origin are unlikely to provide for the inner child within the adult, we need to strengthen the ability to parent ourselves. We need to envision inner parents who carry the qualities of parenting we need and can therefore help the inner child from within. This process can be lonely. The fortunate minority can have long-term therapy where the therapist witnesses and accompanies this important development. Where initial parenting has been inadequate, we may need to call on the positive qualities of the parent archetypes to strengthen our inner self-nurturing abilities. We can use the combination of crown/root/heart chakra energies to link with the archetypes and to bring the healing parent flow into our natural energy system.

Cooperative family healing, such as that which eventually took place in Thomas's family (see case study, page 86), is not always possible. No matter what overtures we make, they may be rejected, misunderstood or simply not recognized. Before it can be worked on cooperatively, all parties have to acknowledge that a problem exists. Sometimes, all we can do as individuals is to change our attitude or perspective and heal ourselves inwardly. When we do this, we gradually become free of the power of the octopus to hold us in negative patterns and free of the model of negative, self-fulfilling prophecies.

FRIENDS, LOVERS AND COLLEAGUES

Blending the energies of crown, heart and root chakras lays a foundation for inner freedom and empowerment. This will not only affect our relationship with our family of origin, but will flood over into all our relationships. When we speak of a persons' heart being 'in the right place' in chakra terms, it means that it is well connected to the root/crown flow. Such people make deep and lasting friendships and relationships. They are reliable colleagues and often, in a subtle way, positively affect relationships in the workplace.

The chakras are more than a system. They are a family in their own right. Practising chakra exercises means that your chakra family begins to work in cooperative harmony. The particular work specified in this chapter, and in Chapters 5 and 7, will help you to become a warm, empowered and heart-centred person who finds fewer complications in relationships and has deeper resources with which to heal or review difficulties. The combined work on self will mean that unreal expectations, and the tendency to seek partnerships or love for the wrong reasons, will recede as your body, emotions and spirit achieve a stronger alignment.

The tie-cutting exercise on page 99 can be used to heal your friendships, your love life and work life as well as your immediate family relationships.

EXERCISES

Exercise 12
Energetically Connecting the Crown/Root/Heart Trio

For this exercise it is better to sit in an upright chair, adopt a cross-legged or lotus position, or to stand.

- Begin by practising central column breathing (see page 17). When you feel that you have become focused and in alignment, direct your attention towards your heart chakra.
- Breathe into the petals of your heart chakra and out through the stem for four or five in/out breath sequences.
- Breathe into your heart chakra, holding the breath in its centre, then breathe up and out through the crown chakra. Breathe in at the crown chakra, bring the breath down to the heart chakra and breathe out through the petals of the heart. Repeat this sequence for four or five in/out breath sequences.
- Breathe into your heart chakra, holding the breath in its centre, then breathe down and out through the root chakra. Breathe in at the root chakra, bring the breath up to the heart chakra and breathe out though the petals of the heart. Repeat this sequence for four or five in/out breath sequences.
- Breathe into your heart chakra, holding the breath in its

centre, then imagine the breath energy going both down to the root and up to the crown as you breathe out through your nose. Repeat this sequence for four or five in/out breath sequences.

Exercise 13
Healing the Inner Child

Before you begin this exercise, consider which aspect of parenting you most lacked as a child. What did you require from your father which he was unable to give? What did you require from your mother which she was unable to give? If you identify many aspects, work with one at a time. Therefore use this exercise progressively as you feel healing taking place.

- Making sure that you will be undisturbed, practise central column breathing (see page 17). Bring the breath rhythm into your heart chakra . . . As you breathe in and out through the petals of your heart, imagine a warm, rose-pink colour permeating your heart chakra . . .
- Now imagine your inner child, in your heart chakra, surrounded by this warm, rose-pink colour . . . Be aware of the needs of your inner child . . .
- If your inner child lacked father qualities, whilst still holding the child in the rose-pink of your heart centre, imagine a flow of energy, carrying the lacking qualities, coming into your heart from your crown chakra . . . This flow is coming from the Great Father towards your inner child with tenderness and healing . . . Let the rose-pink colour of your heart and your tender holding of your inner child in your heart chakra enable the healing energy from the Great Father to be received . . .
- If your inner child lacked mother qualities, whilst still holding the child in the rose-pink of your heart centre,

imagine a flow of energy, carrying the lacking qualities, coming into your heart from your root chakra . . . This flow of energy is coming from the Great Mother towards your inner child, with tenderness and healing . . . Let the rose-pink colour of your heart and your tender holding of your inner child in your heart chakra enable the healing energy from the Great Mother to be received . . .

Exercise 14
Cutting the Ties that Bind

This exercise will help to heal any negative links to your family of origin, friends, lovers or colleagues, and enable the purer energy of the acceptance of karmic purpose and true heart love to bring about healing on an energetic level.

To be effective, tie-cutting visualizations need to be repeated frequently (daily or every other day) for about a month. They should then be repeated about once a week until a difference is noticed, and thereafter used from time to time as reinforcement or if similar situations or old-style reactions recur. Getting a friend, partner or counsellor to 'witness' your intention in cutting the ties can be a great help. If you want to cut the ties with more than one person, make a separate visualization for each. If there are more than two people or situations to deal with, first select the two most vital ones to work on. Start new visualizations only after you have worked for approximately two months with the original ones.

Either select one of the following methods for use, or use each of them alternately.

Method 1

- Begin with central column breathing (see page 17) and then breathe in and out through your heart chakra.
- Visualize yourself standing in a circle of light. The person with whom you wish to cut the ties is also standing in a circle of light, facing you. Your circles of light are touching each other or even slightly overlapping. There are greyish pulsating cords running from some of your vital centres or chakras to the corresponding centres in the other person. (These most commonly run from root chakra to root chakra, sacral to sacral, solar plexus to solar plexus.)
- In your visualization move back so that your circles no longer overlap; now put an extra circle of violet light around your existing circle and then a fine circle of silver light around that. Do the same for the person with whom you are intending to cut the ties. Emphasize the space between your circles.
- Now visualize the grey cords withering and dropping away into the space between you. Let the space between you become a river of light. The river of light takes the cords into its flow, filling them with light and washing them away to the sea.
- Ask your guardian angel for a blessing, and ask the other person's guardian angel to do the same for them. As you bask in the light of blessing, try to become aware of the lessons that you and the other person have taught or mirrored to each other and be thankful for those lessons.
- Feel your own space firmly around you as you let the visualization fade.

Method 2

- Begin with central column breathing (see page 17) and then breathe in and out through your heart chakra.
- Visualize yourself standing opposite the person with whom you wish to cut the ties. Visualize a symbol of peace

which you would wish to offer to this person, and see them holding it. See yourself holding a replica of this symbol. As you hold the symbols, be aware of the lessons you have reflected for each other.

- As in Method 1, see the grey and pulsating cords which bind, running between your vital areas or chakras. Visualize a shaft of silver light, which flashes three times between you, melting away the cords and leaving you free.
- See a pathway of light behind you and behind the person with whom you are cutting the ties. See each of you turn, with your symbol of peace, to follow your own distinctive path. As you walk away, the shaft of light appears to define a boundary. In future neither of you can cross that boundary except at the other's invitation. (This method is particularly good where there has been a sense of 'invasion' by another person.)

THE COLOURS

The main colours for the heart chakra are spring green, rose and rose amethyst.

Spring green is the colour of young beech leaves in early spring. It is a delicate colour linking to the key word of tenderness.

Positively, green is the colour of spring, growth, opening and permission to move forward. It helps to heal the pain which comes from being over-vulnerable to life and to open the heart when it has 'hardened' as a result of opposition or devastating emotional experiences.

Negatively, it may be considered to be unlucky. (Older types of green paint contained lead and led to ill-health and poisoning.) It is also the colour of jealousy – 'green with envy'.

Rose is a gentle rose-pink; rose quartz crystals give the right depth and quality for this heart colour.

Positively, rose is a warm colour, also indicating tenderness and delicacy of approach. It brings warmth and softness and is comforting to the bereaved.

Negatively, it may be rather sickly-sweet and produce a vibration of discord.

Rose amethyst is a deeper rose colour, with a touch of mauve or amethyst in it, making it a bluer pink. It is linked to the key word of detachment in the heart chakra.

Positively, rose amethyst helps to lead us towards wisdom and is strengthening to the heart after debilitating illnesses or in stress conditions. It balances blood pressure.

Negatively, it can become the colour of too cold, over-clinical detachment.

Follow the directions for Exercise 8, page 42, for breathing these colours into your heart chakra to develop and strengthen it.

THE FRAGRANCES

Sandalwood and rose quieten the heart chakra, while pine and honeysuckle stimulate it. If you sense that your heart is too open and that you tend to put other people's needs before your own, then use sandalwood and rose. If you find it difficult to express your feelings, or are hesitant about touching and being touched, you will benefit from using pine and honeysuckle. Look back to your reflections on the heart chakra question on page 80 to get a sense of which of these fragrances will benefit you most.

See page 43 for suggestions for using the fragrances. Also consider making a balancing blend of one stimulating and one quietening fragrance from each of the root, crown and heart chakras. This will help to establish and energize the root/ crown/heart trio.

The Crystals

Refer to page 44 and the Glossary for general guidance on using crystals. The crystals which will best help the issues considered in this chapter are:

Ruby To vitalize, nourish and warm. This is the stone to use for healing when there has been a difficult birth or where bonding of the baby to the mother has been delayed for some reason.

Rose Quartz To encourage self-nurturing and bring the quality of warm, unconditional, motherly love to heal all who have had too little of this in their lives.

Green Calcite To vitalize all our subtle bodies, but particularly the feeling body. This helps the communication between head and heart, brings strength during periods of change and transition, heals the wounds of the heart and encourages the development of positive tenderness.

Amber All shades of amber resonate with the heart chakra. It purifies and helps to develop balance and love.

Prayers or Affirmations

The root chakra prayer or affirmation is:

> Through incarnation may spirit be brought into matter. Through rootedness may life-force be recharged and exchanged. We acknowledge wholeness and seek to gain and to reflect acceptance.

The crown chakra prayer or affirmation is:

> Through surrender and release let the incoming will be truly the will of God working within us and through us, leading us increasingly to knowledge of mystical union and mystical marriage.

The heart chakra prayer or affirmation is:

> In the golden centre of the rose of the heart may tender
> compassion be linked to unconditional love. May true
> detachment enable growth and continuity. Through the
> understanding of birth within death and death within
> birth may there be transformation.

For suggestions on using prayers or affirmations, see page 45.

Chapter 5

Affairs of the Heart:
Love and Passion

Key Issues: Passion, Tenderness
Chakra Pair: Root and Heart
Archetype: Love

This chapter will help you to:
- love life on earth
- understand and combine the qualities of passion and tenderness
- have a fuller appreciation of natural beauty
- understand better and live more effectively with the law of love within the universe

---

For lists of the areas of influence see page 19 for the root chakra and page 77 for the heart chakra.

THE ROOT AND HEART AS A CHAKRA PAIR

In Chapter 4 we looked at the root, heart and crown chakras as a trio but the energy link between the root and heart as a pair is also significant. We have seen how the heart chakra brings in the dimension of relationship. In the trio with root and crown, its main influence is on our relationship to our karmic task and our family of origin. When *paired* with the root it enables us fully to relate to the earth and to feel the passions which are one of the gifts of human experience. The sacral/ heart link (to be explored in Chapter 6) is also connected with passion, but more directly to sexual passion and the passions of power and empowerment.

The root/heart connection gives us a love of beauty, harmony and comfort and inspires us to high ideals in these areas. When the link between root and heart chakras is clear, our living on earth, our use of its resources and our relationships with each other are as though blessed by the goddess. If the collective root/heart connection were in order we would be unable to:

- blot the landscape with ugly buildings
- pollute the rivers and the soil
- use negative, violence-generating, sounds or rhythms in our music
- feel violence or hatred towards each other
- misuse the world's resources
- be motivated by greed and envy
- be unconscious of our natural responsibilities
- see our times of incarnation on earth as some kind of exile
- sow the seeds of discontent
- suffer from loss of meaning
- be without love

In short, we would all be united in working towards a utopian society. Yet, moving away from idealism, if we look at the above list on an individual basis, it can be seen that the root/heart connection has the potential to heal many of the areas of unease and discontent to which most of us fall victim from time to time.

Because a major part of our evolution is worked out through earth incarnation, we need the root chakra. It enables us to be in our bodies, to adapt to the vibrations of matter, to have the instinct to fulfil our basic needs, and to deal with the material world. On its own, it merely enables us to live and to be aware of our physiological needs. In its links to other chakras it plays its part in enabling us to be healthy, wealthy and wise.

PASSION

When root is linked to heart, we can feel a passion for life which motivates us to deepen our experiences. Rather than having the feeling of just 'passing through', we become, not only voluntarily, but passionately, resident here. We begin to care, not only for ourselves, our immediate families or our race, but for each other as members of the total family of humanity. We not only conceive visions of higher ideals and values but we work towards them. We do not sit back and moan whilst others govern and make decisions – instead we insist on becoming a part of the decision-making mechanisms. We become witnesses for each other, in the sense of being mutual reminders that we should refuse to accept less than the best, not from vanity, but from a healthy sense of self-worth and because we believe in a high potential for humanity.

Gildas, along with many other guides, has long assured us that we are on the brink of entering a new and golden age. One of the most potent things we can do, to help us more towards this state of new awareness, is to work on connecting the heart and root chakras. When the connection is made we do not have to *try* to be better human beings than we are; the energy which prevents us being anything other than a true and passionate world citizen actually flows through our subtle energy systems, positively affecting our beliefs and actions.

TENDERNESS

In Chapter 4 we also saw that the capacity of the heart for tenderness is a major factor in bringing about relationship. Tenderness can also mean vulnerability. The root chakra gives us instinctual, survival strengths but, without moderating factors, these would remain at a rather primitive, neanderthal level. To the neanderthal human, tenderness could have been a threat to survival. Yet because, as a species, we have evolved into greater consciousness, we are now in a position where we may need tenderness and vulnerability to help keep the wisdom of our instincts alive. The development of the mind and our ability to find mechanical solutions to most material problems can mask a necessary awareness of vulnerability. There is, of course, a vicious circle, since our initial vulnerability stimulated the mechanical creativity which is now in danger of masking our natural instincts. Tenderness, which is an antidote to force, can help us preserve our instincts without denying our powers of mind and creativity.

When we have a more tender relationship with earth we respect its life-force and release the nurturer or the mother goddess within it (see also pages 94, 95 and 98) without setting ourselves up in opposition or conflict with that which is natural. With tenderness we can be responsive without becoming negatively vulnerable. The art of linking and exchanging energies between root and heart chakras can enable this shift and resolution.

Case Study: Affairs of the Heart

Sharon could not form lasting relationships, yet her main passion in life, as a successful journalist, was an interest in people. An only child, she described her childhood as one where she was technically well-provided for and loved. Her father worked as a freelance radio broadcaster and journalist. When he had fulfilled a good contract or been well paid for an article, he and her mother would 'get on a high' and take sudden trips by car to France, a country they both loved. Within hours they would be ready to depart. Sharon found that she let friends down, when plans had been made, or missed things she had been looking forward to at school. She felt temperamentally different from her parents and their mood swings but learned not to make commitments in case they could not be honoured. When her father was not doing well he would become withdrawn, depressed and prone to drown his sorrows in drink. As a situation developed which made Sharon feel she could never invite anyone home, she increasingly held people at arm's length.

When Sharon was fourteen her mother contracted a long-term degenerative illness. On the surface her father dealt with this well and, as the illness got worse, was an attentive carer and nurse. But at an emotional level Sharon felt that her father did not cope at all. Later she had understood that the only way he could deal with his feelings was to deny them.

His drinking became heavier and he encouraged his sick wife to drink with him whenever she became depressed about her condition. Few outsiders or relatives realized it, since most of the drinking was in private, but eventually Sharon was living with two alcoholics. There was no violence. Her father became maudlin when drunk and her mother would just withdraw and sleep, but everything in the household was unpredictable and disorganized. She learned not to ask for help, understanding that the family secret must be kept. Sharon was eighteen when, at last, her father faced some of his need and vulnerability and asked his unmarried sister to move in. Sharon had just been accepted as a cub reporter on a local newspaper. She moved into a flat of her own so that she could live a more ordered life.

The insecure, Bohemian existence with strong emotional undercurrents denied at surface level, and the pathos of her parents' dilemma, together with her mother's early death, had caused Sharon to withdraw into herself. She felt cold and clinical inside. Some of her journalistic writing showed passion but she was concerned that, often, when other reporters were moved by the life situations they had to confront, she stayed not only detached but unaffected.

In many ways Sharon was an attractive woman of the world. She was not short of male escorts but somehow nothing ever seemed to develop into the loving relationship she longed for. She was seeking help now, because her latest boyfriend, in parting from her, had described her as a 'cold, calculating, ice-maiden'.

At a psychological level there was relatively long-term work to be done on resurrecting and understanding the feelings from Sharon's childhood. Through an 'alternative therapies' page in the newspaper for which she worked, Sharon had become interested in chakras and the spiritual approach. She wanted self-help tools.

Soon Sharon understood that the connection between her heart and root chakras had had little chance of forming. She began to work with these chakras separately and also with the breathing exercise for the transformative link. She felt that this energetic work enabled her to change some things quite quickly and also that it sustained her during the painful process of finding the feelings she had needed to deny in order to survive. Before her therapy was finished she had found a new male partner and was contemplating the big step, especially for her, of moving in with him.

THE ARCHETYPE: LOVE

This archetype has been chosen for this chapter because I believe it to be the basic law on which the universe is founded. Establishing the flow between the root and heart chakras brings love in its highest forms into manifestation.

In the English language we have only one word for love and it has become very overworked. Other languages, particularly ancient Greek, provide words for gradations of love. *Filios* is family love; *Eros* is erotic or romantic love; *Agape* (literally translated as 'the love feast') is the love which comes from mutuality and spiritual communion. This last probably comes closest to that which Gildas describes as an archetype in process of being born: the archetype of unconditional love. He names one of the 'new' chakras as The Unconditional Love Centre (see page 243), and describes it as a deeper opening of the heart. To enable that deeper opening and the connection to the chakra and archetype of unconditional love the root/heart links first need to be strengthened. Gildas sees trust as essential to the flow of love:

Trust that 'all is well, all manner of things are well and all shall be very well indeed'. Such trust casts out fear and allows love to flow in. Love enables, creates and transforms. Even, and especially in the face of all your current difficulties on earth, practise love more consistently in your inner and outer lives. Give it out and allow it to flow in. It is the life-force of change.

EXERCISES

Exercise 15
Linking Root and Heart Energies

This is the basic exercise for making a connection between your root and heart chakras. Besides strengthening and harmonizing your energy body, it will help you to be more positive in your approach to life; to heal or balance any negative feelings you have towards yourself or others; strengthen your resistance to atmospheric pollution of all kinds, including noise pollution; give you a clearer sense of responsibility; link you to the Source of All Life; improve your access to contentment; aid your search for meaning; enable you to be more loving to others and to be more receptive to love from others.

- Begin with central column breathing (see page 17). When you feel ready to do so, breathe in and out at your heart centre, keeping a natural breath rhythm.
- Now breathe in through the petals of the heart chakra, hold the breath in its centre for a count of three, then breathe down into the root chakra and out deeply into the earth. (Practise this for ten in-out breath sequences.)
- Change to breathing in from the earth, into the root chakra, holding the breath in the centre of the root chakra for a count of three, then breathe on up into the centre of the heart chakra and out through the heart petals. (Practise this for ten in-out breaths.)
- Re-establish your own normal, relaxed, breathing pattern.

Exercise 16
A Love Meditation

- Make sure that you will be undisturbed and begin with the usual practice of central column breathing (see page 17), gradually focusing into finding a natural rhythm of breathing in and out through your heart chakra.
- Imagine a cosmic source of love-light just above the crown of your head . . . As you breathe in, draw love into your body from this source. . . Imagine it permeating each bodily area . . . Imagine it flowing through your blood vessels and vitalizing your cells . . . Imagine your whole body glowing with the light of love . . . Continue to breathe love-light into your own body and being on each in-breath,

and on each out-breath breathe it into the atmosphere
around you . . . Breathe it into the earth, the furniture,
the walls and ceilings and all the physical substance of your
home . . . Send it out to loved ones and to your pets . . .
Breathe it into your plants, your garden, the substance of
earth itself . . . Sense that each particle which begins to
glow with this love-light passes its luminosity on to whatever
is next to it . . . The glow of love in the earth goes deeper
and deeper . . . The love-light in each person touches that
in another . . . Imagine the whole planet and all its peoples
bathed in the light of love, causing everything to flourish
in peak health and vitality . . .

- When you are ready to do so, come back gently to your
everyday surroundings. As you go about your tasks,
continue to carry a sense of the love-light with you . . . Let
it be there, subtly, to touch all whom you meet.

THE COLOURS

The colours for the root chakra are red, brown and mauve;
and, for the heart chakra, spring green, rose and rose amethyst.
To strengthen the colours in your root and heart chakras, refer
to Exercise 8 (page 42).

THE FRAGRANCES

For the root chakra the quietening fragrances are cedarwood
and patchouli, and the stimulating ones are musk, lavender and
hyacinth. For the heart chakra the quietening fragrances are
sandalwood and rose, and the stimulating ones are pine and
honeysuckle. See page 43 for suggestions for using the fragrances.

For strengthening and balancing the root/heart connection choose one stimulating and one quietening fragrance for each chakra, then blend the oils together to make a balancing essence.

THE CRYSTALS

Refer to page 44 and the Glossary for general guidance on using crystals. The crystals which will best help the issues considered in this chapter are:

Watermelon Tourmaline. To aid tolerance, flexibility, compassion and transformation. Watermelon tourmaline helps the heart chakra to open and to maintain the sort of flexibility which keeps it healthy.

Apache Tears. These are small, tear-shaped pieces of black obsidian. They promote tenderness but also help us to link to the natural cycles of the earth. They strengthen our ability to link instinct with creativity.

PRAYERS OR AFFIRMATIONS

The root chakra prayer or affirmation is:

> Through incarnation may spirit be brought into matter.
> Through rootedness may life-force be recharged and
> exchanged. We acknowledge wholeness and seek to gain
> and to reflect acceptance.

The heart chakra prayer or affirmation is:

> In the golden centre of the rose of the heart may tender
> compassion be linked to unconditional love. May true
> detachment enable growth and continuity. Through the

understanding of birth within death and death within birth may there be transformation.

For suggestions on using prayers or affirmations, see page 45.

Chapter 6

The Life-Force:
Sex, Power and Creativity

Key Issues: Sex, Violence, Creativity, Romance, Enduring Love, Power Games, Empowerment, Power, Abundance

Chakra Pairs: Sacral and Root, Sacral and Heart

Chakra Triad: Sacral, Root and Heart

Archetypes: Creativity, Peace, Sexuality, Power and Abundance

---

This chapter will help you to:
- **release blockages around sex, money and authority**
- **understand more about violence and its relationship to creativity**
- **take another step towards owning your own power**
- **learn more about the nature of abundance**

AREAS OF INFLUENCE

For lists of the areas of influence see page 19 for the root chakra and page 77 for the heart chakra.

The Sacral Chakra:

Location The petals are approximately two fingers below the navel. The stem corresponds to the sacrum area of the spine.
Key Words Security, Sense of Others, Sexuality, Creativity, Empowerment, Co-creativity, Sincerity
Developmental Age 3/5–8yrs
Colours Orange, Amber, Gold (non-metallic)
Element Water
Sense Taste
Body Etheric
Glandular Connection Lymphatics
Quietening Fragrances Musk, Amber
Stimulating Fragrances Rosemary, Rose Geranium
Crystals and Gemstones Amber, Citrine, Topaz, Aventurine, Moonstone, Jasper

Prayer or Affirmation

May the unity of humanity with each other and the earth enable true creativity. May release from a sense of sin and unworthiness lead us into the full knowledge of our empowerment as co-creators, at one with, and a part of the Divine.

SACRAL AND ROOT AS A CHAKRA PAIR

The developmental stage for the sacral chakra is 3/5–8yrs. The variation in the lower age as a starting point for the age most developmentally linked to this chakra is partly generational. The modern baby develops much faster than a baby of thirty years or more ago was encouraged to do. Thus wider issues become important at an earlier age. It will always, whatever the generation, depend to a large extent on individual development, but if you are over thirty it is likely that your sacral chakra stage would have started at around the age of five. If you are younger than twenty then it will more probably have started at around three. Looking back to these ages will give you a fuller insight into the emotional and physical factors affecting your chakra's development.

Linked to the sense of taste, the element of water and the lymphatic glands, the sacral chakra in its own right affects, and is affected by, our emotional mood swings, our preferences (not only in foods but in the broad sense of the tastes and fashions of life), our symbolic relationship to flow and fluidity, our fertility or fecundity and the surges of our sexual awareness and desires. The question to ask yourself at the sacral chakra is: 'How do I taste the world and how does the world taste me?'

When a chakra is studied in isolation or as an individual member of the full team, then understanding its full range of areas of influence is the primary aim. In considering the energetic links formed by pairs and trios of chakras, the intensity of relationship between the centres affects the original key words by creating key *issues*. In viewing the sacral chakra in conjunction with the root and heart, the key issues become: sexuality, creativity, co-creativity, violence, power, empowerment, romantic and enduring love, wealth, abundance and poverty. The issues most linked to the root/sacral pair are sexuality, creativity, co-creativity, violence, power, empowerment, wealth, abundance and poverty.

We have seen that the root chakra, with its element of earth, supplies the energetic force which enables us to live on earth and to deal with our bodies and the material world. The sacral chakra also, through the etheric body and the element of water, closely interacts with the material plane. Earth, at the root chakra, gives fixity and stability. Water, at the sacral, brings a sense of movement. Water is linked to the moon. Symbolically it is often interpreted as governing the emotions. Inevitably it connects with time and tide, to fertility cycles, to the patterns of menstruation and ovulation in women and the production of seminal fluid in men.

Earth and water define each other. Watercourses cut their way even through the bed-rock of earth but the earth contains them. Without water, earth is infertile and inert. With it, earth becomes alive and productive. The element of water at the sacral chakra also means that it is linked to bodily fluids such as the life-force of blood, the hydration of the body, and the fluid processes of cleansing and elimination.

Symbolically, this consideration of the interaction of the elements of water and earth teaches us a great deal about the relationship between the sacral and the root. Water needs the containment of earth, but without water earth becomes infertile and inert. Blood is life-force and the blood is fluid. The sacral chakra, then, imbues our incarnation and evolution with life-force. Apart from the general vitality which flows through us, our most potent connection to life-force is our ability to procreate and reproduce the species. Around our consciousness of this ability many powerful issues arise. They mostly accumulate around the emotive subject of sex.

Sex and Sexuality

Sex, as an instinctual drive for the furtherance of the species, belongs to the root chakra. Sexuality covers a much wider field. If earth is the containing substance for watercourses, then sex alone is the coursing of the waters, whilst sexuality is the interaction between the earth and the flowing water. It is a term which covers all aspects of gender, sexual awareness and procreation.

As the family of humanity has increased and communications have become more sophisticated, we have studied ourselves and our behaviour patterns. We are aware of concerns such as world population and its increases, decreases and distribution in relationship to world resources. We study matters of sexual potency, fertility and contraception. Using the latter, we endeavour to control patterns of population and their relationship to national or world economy. Fashions and expectations, as to the accepted size of a family, keep changing. We develop social mores and, as individuals, demand the right to make decisions about our sexual behaviours and orientation. We practise sexual intercourse and the stimulation of orgasm as an art, seeing it not only as signifying a special relationship with another human being but as a deep and intimate expression of love.

From this consciousness of sexual power and the strong motivating instinct within it, much confusion and many double standards have arisen. For Western cultures the strict morality of Victorian times actually and figuratively pushed sex into the closet. Although today there is a comparative openness about sexual behaviour and desires, it can be very difficult for a young person reaching puberty to obtain good sexual teaching and information. Often the family, which would seem the best environment in which to learn and be guided about intimate matters, is a place where sexual matters are avoided or approached with such embarrassment that only minimal knowledge is given. Information given in the school classroom may prepare young people for puberty, explain the mysteries of wet dreams, voice changes and shaving for boys, the management of menstruation for girls, the facts of sexual intercourse and the making of babies for both, but all too often this is where it stops. Full discussion of sex as an art, or of the force of bodily and emotional feelings which sexual awakening engenders, is rare. Unprejudiced, supervised opportunities for openness about homosexuality and sexual orientation are even rarer.

Despite all our knowledge, and our desire to shape and control ourselves and our world, we plunge, or are plunged, into our sexual lives, either to learn from painful experience or to acquire inhibitions which last for the rest of our lives. It is sad that such a situation exists when this is the very area of life in which we can find and acknowledge our most potent sense of co-creatorship. With feelings of passion, tenderness and orgasmic experience, we can reproduce ourselves and experience the joy of giving birth to, and nurturing, another being.

Since we have gained knowledge about fertility cycles and mechanical means of contraception it has also been more possible, within relationships, to explore sex as a celebration of our existence and as an expression of mutual love. Gildas teaches that sex which is deliberately 'not an invitation to another soul to incarnate' can channel our passions to enhance and feed our joy in life and our natural creativity for other projects. When we do not understand this more subtle fertility which we can give each other, and feel that continence or abstinence are virtues in themselves, then full understanding of ourselves as co-creators within the universe is clouded.

Lack of sexual knowledge, together with shame and inhibition about our sexuality, lead to the growth of the shadow side of sex. Promiscuity, rape, pornography, power issues and true sexual perversions become rabid social problems. In our intimate areas we feel ourselves to be most piteously at risk. We carry a corporate wound. It is not difficult to account, symbolically, for the current prevalence of AIDS, the sexually transmitted auto-immune disease.

We can help our bodies and our emotions to achieve greater harmony with our sexual drives and practices by working with the sacral and root chakras as an energy pair. When the energy flow between these two chakras is fully connected and freely flowing we can become guilt-free about our sexuality and in the control or focus of powerful urges. Thus it becomes easier for us to happily practise self-release (masturbation), continence or abstinence when necessary, learn to better respect sexual drives and orientation in ourselves and others, celebrate our sexuality as a co-creative power and exciting expression of our love for a partner, consciously rejoice in the joy of procreation and physicality, and aid the healing of any sexual, or sexually linked, physical or emotional dysfunction (see page 143 for Exercise 17, Linking Root and Sacral Energies).

Co-creativity, Empowerment, Creativity and Violence

Procreation is our primary area of co-creativity. Whatever our spiritual or metaphysical beliefs, the mystery of the creation of humanity is central and enduring. If we and other living species in the universe have been created by some divine power or explosive creative force, then embodied within us is the ability to reproduce ourselves. This must be seen as a reflection of a universe which is continually in the process of 'becoming'.

If we can reproduce ourselves, then we also create, mould or condition ourselves and the world in which we live. Currently we are experiencing the flip-side of much of what we have brought into being. As we learn from this, and reap the harvest which tells us that we need to do better, the Divine Principles or higher archetypes constantly reassert themselves (see Chapter 2, page 23). As we give attention to this reassertion, so our awareness of the privilege and empowerment of co-creativity within the universe also impinges strongly upon us. We see the laws of cause and effect fully enacted within and around us. An awesome responsibility dawns and we are required to grow beyond power, into empowerment.

Power is a *principle* and empowerment is the *process* of making use of that principle. Psychological empowerment is about having access to all our capabilities and not waiting for permission or approval from others in order to use them. The truly empowered person has overcome negative conditioning and authority issues, is free to be creative, and uses his or her creativity to empower others.

A phrase often used in groups dedicated to self-help or self-growth is 'giving away your power'. When other people, parents, teachers, society or outer authorities are seen as manipulative, judgmental or limiting, it is possible that we are *giving* them this power. We may be *allowing* them unreasonably to influence our adult choices and make unjustified demands on our time and resources. When others are set on a pedestal and made into gurus or invincible leaders, our own roles are limited to those of disciples or followers. If the idol is discovered to have feet of clay, distress can be great and the recovery period long. The empowered person respects the authority, wisdom or expertise of another without self-belittlement and becomes more empowered by the contact. True teachers and leaders seek to empower others and to work towards their own redundancy. They do not seek glamour or applause for its own sake. When we respect multiplicity of talents and celebrate each other's gifts, rather than feeling jealous or devalued by what others have, we can work towards mutual empowerment in every human relationship and contact.

Creativity is not simply about being artistic or able to make beautiful objects, but about living creatively. We may be totally unable to wield a paintbrush, use colour well, write poetry or prose, cook, sew or produce other handicrafts, yet be creative in living. We may be problem-solvers, good at relationships and mediation, inspired home-makers, appreciators of beauty or nature, in tune with incarnation, or skilled in the art of compromise and creative decision-making. The creative person maintains an ability to play, is not afraid to take risks, sustains a belief in magic, and delights in a sense of wonder. The golden child is alive and nurtured within. (For more on this, see *The River of Life*, details in the Bibliography.)

Violence often comes from frustrated sexuality and creativity. If we accept that sexual energies come from the urge to create and that violence often erupts when the creative force is unchannelled, we must look carefully at the relationship between these energies within ourselves as well as within society as a whole. Many of us turn anger or violence inwards. Rather than join the football hooligans or vandals, we inwardly destroy our own sense of worth.

When we have little sense of self-value we get stuck in dead-end situations, seeing no way out and entering the downward energy spiral of misery and depression (see page 144 for Exercise 18, Correcting the Downward Energy Spiral). This downward energy spiral is also a series of vicious circles. If our environment and circumstances are dreary we identify with them and so increasingly reflect back to ourselves that we are no good and unworthy. Anger can be a valuable catalyst in this situation. Becoming angry about our situation, the way others are treating us, or our lack of opportunity can signal the birth of self-value and respect.

If we can use the word 'outrageous' about the things which block us, then we are on our way to being able to convert our anger into creative action. We may also need to use much stronger language to express our anger and allow ourselves to stamp, scream, punch, thump and shout our rage, but within the word 'outrageous' there is the dawning of non-identification with those aspects of our lot in life which have made us feel so separated or underprivileged. 'Outrageous' says 'I am worth more'; 'Things can get better'; 'I am on the brink of change'; 'My potential to live creatively is awakening'. At a wider level it also says: 'The human condition can be improved'; 'If we work together, we can create a better society for the whole family of humanity'. The spiral exercise on page 144 may awaken any dormant sense of outrage within you. Remember that it is often the necessary prelude to the release of creative energy for life-change.

The following case study illustrates some of the ways in which frustrated creativity, sexuality and violence can interact in our lives.

Case Study: The Creative Life-Force

Living in a one-roomed flat in a near derelict house in a down-at-heel area of an inner city, Elizabeth had never really found her way in life. An only child, when she was five years old, her mother had left the marital home, taking Elizabeth with her. Shortly afterwards her parents divorced. Her father failed to make any regular arrangements to continue contact with her. His reluctance to put himself out to look after her as a child made Elizabeth conclude that she was of little interest or concern to him.

Her mother was a career woman and had a well-paid job. The financial aspects of being a single parent were not particularly pressing. Nevertheless Elizabeth was affected not only by the disruption and bewilderment of the divorce and separation from her father but by her mother's emotional turmoil and series of relationships with unsuitable men. From an early age Elizabeth began to think negatively about herself. Although she was extremely intelligent she had always under-achieved, usually joining the trouble-makers and drop-outs within the school system. Not knowing what she really wanted to do with her life, she acquired a few secretarial skills, left school and home early, lived in a bedsit, and had a series of low-paid, unstimulating jobs.

She eventually drifted into a relationship with an unemployed man, and moved in with him, to a house shared with two other out-of-work couples. Her partner and the others in the house were all musical and artistic. Elizabeth felt that she was moving into an environment where she might develop a talent she knew she had for poetry and artistic illustration. She, too, gave up work and began claiming benefits.

Elizabeth had a passionate nature and had had previous sexual experience. Initially, making love with her first live-in partner was exciting and fulfilling. In the Bohemian environment she had moved into, she felt that her artistic side was being brought out and inspired. Yet, gradually, things began to go wrong. Elizabeth discovered that she could not maintain her own space in a full-time relationship. A naturally fastidious person, the condition of the shared living conditions, especially the bathroom, became daunting. No one except herself seemed to care about cleanliness or order. Because they were all unemployed they were always in each other's way. Even the room she shared with her partner became claustrophobic. Although those around her were certainly artistically and musically gifted, they were unmotivated when it came to thoroughly practising or channelling their gifts. The vision she had glimpsed of developing her own talent in a supportive community situation shifted and died.

In these conditions Elizabeth's sense of self, already fragile, plunged to a new low. She became despondent and lethargic. Her partner, basically creatively frustrated, wanted her to experiment with some sexual variations which she found distasteful. He became sexually importunate and eventually violent towards her, destroying the last vestiges of passion and joy in the relationship. At this point Elizabeth found enough energy and sense of self-preservation to move out into a small flat lent to her by a friend who had gone abroad. She was still living there when she came to me and had been through a period of overwhelming loneliness, suicidal depression and despair. She had eventually glimpsed a chink of light at the end of the tunnel when, visiting a local market, she had bumped into one of her former drop-out/troublemaker friends from her schooldays. The friend was now happily married. She had taken a silver-smithing course and produced her own jewellery which she sold at various markets and craft fairs.

The friend saw Elizabeth's dilemma and, concerned for her, invited her to come to her home. Eventually Elizabeth began to help on her friend's market stall. The friend had also become interested in yoga and, from that, in chakras and the spiritual approach to life. She lent Elizabeth one of my books and eventually they came to a workshop when I was visiting their part of the country. After the workshop Elizabeth asked me for some personal help with working with her chakras. She also realized that she needed some long-term counselling to help her deal with the enormous rages she had begun to experience and which often frightened her with their intensity.

She worked with a local counsellor and visited me from

time to time. It took a while for Elizabeth's rage to turn to outrage at what life had done to her, but when it did she quickly realized how to channel the energy of the anger into initiating changes for herself. She continued to help with her friend's jewellery marketing, which was now becoming so successful that she could be paid for what she did and gradually come off state benefits. She took a part-time art course to build up a portfolio and was eventually successful in getting a place on a foundation year and then an art degree course.

Although her relationship with her parents had been very tenuous for some years, both her father and her mother rallied round when she approached them, and supported her financially so that she could do the training of her choice.

Elizabeth valued the way in which her long-term counselling helped her to have insights and to find her inner strength, but she always maintained that the work with her chakras was a vital force in enabling her to pull back from her lowest points. She found the spiral exercise (page 144) particularly valuable in balancing her sexual and creative energies and combating depression.

SACRAL AND HEART AS A CHAKRA PAIR

The flow from the physiological and primal needs of the root chakra, into power, empowerment, sexuality, passion, creativity and greater consciousness, at the sacral, means that the sacral is the main energetic seat of the emotions. Given a reasonably free and encouraging environment, the young child is a passionate being. The developmental age for the sacral chakra covers the time in which we struggle with aspects of power, authority and dominance. To handle the temper tantrums of the three-year-old, give the necessary boundaries and yet leave the child with a sense of empowerment is a difficult task indeed. The young child *becomes* its rage. Children's emotions are often bigger than the small being can contain.

The art of emotional maturity is not as simple as learning self-control and the ability to behave appropriately to the occasion or to society's expectations. If the child experiences an emotionally wounding environment, or is disempowered or controlled through over-harsh discipline, the inner child within the adult may be seething with resentment, hostility and rage. Continued attempts by the growing adult to contain, control or repress this aspect of themselves will lead to its gaining ever greater autonomy. That which is pushed down too strenuously into unconsciousness eventually becomes more powerful than, and directly opposes, that which is seemingly determinedly held at the zenith of consciousness. The repressed, passionate child self will eventually and unexpectedly erupt in the most inappropriate situations.

Since, in a sense, the child *is* the emotion, the experience of being 'had' and controlled by emotion will continue into adult experience. The violent action immediately regretted, the words said which we wish unsaid, the bewildered question 'Whatever came over me?' are all indications that true emotional maturity has eluded us in some area of life. In chakra terms such reactions mean that the link between the sacral and the heart needs attention, since the heart is the seat of feeling which is the second, or higher level of emotion (see also Chapters 4 and 9).

If, at the developmental stage of the sacral chakra, all has been reasonably well and conditions have been 'good enough' for the child, then a certain amount of emotional control without repression will have been gained. The child will be in touch with emotion without being overwhelmed by it, but the true conversion of that emotion into the ability to *feel* without being inappropriately *emotional* happens at the heart chakra stage for which the developmental age is 12–15 years (see also page 79).

Entry into adolescence is also a time when we are in touch

with deep emotions, feelings, passions, romantic ideals and the need to 'act out' our fervours. Once again sexuality is at the forefront of life. Our physical bodies change and mature; our hormones become active; drives which may bewilder us assert themselves; and being accepted by our peer group is all-important.

If parents, teachers, the climate in which we live and the primary foundations laid at the sacral chakra are all 'good enough', we come through this period positively with our feeling selves active. We are well on our way to developing tenderness, compassion, and the ability to touch and be touched by the world around us. Our emotions become mellowed by wisdom. 'Acting out' ripens into knowing what we feel but also knowing where and how to channel that feeling without repressing it. We are fully capable of having emotions without being governed and driven by them. A seasoned quality of true feeling emerges which enables us to appreciate the higher principles of life, feel passionate about them and express them wisely in our lives.

Where there are difficulties in the natural development of this most significant link between the sacral and heart chakras, there may be much work for us to do in order to be content with our emotional and feeling lives. Working with the inner child and/or inner adolescent can help the psychological healing process (see also page 91 and Exercises 13 and 28). Energetically, this growth can be initiated, aided and supported by working with the sacral/heart chakra connection (see Exercise 19, page 146).

The Emotional Body

The relationship between sacral and heart chakras introduces another subtle body into the energetic system. This is the emotional body which carries the record of all our emotional development. When the heart chakra is balanced and a sound feeling body is developed, then there is the potential for a good relationship between the emotional and feeling bodies. A balanced emotional body, resulting from working energetically with the sacral/heart connection, lays a strong foundation for healing within the psyche and energy systems.

In recent years the 'stiff upper lip' characteristic of the British has been much criticized. This has led to psychological encouragement for repressed emotions from the past (that which is stored in the emotional body) to be contacted and acted out as an essential part of any full healing or growth process. To some extent this is correct but sometimes it can go too far.

Our lives are difficult when our emotional bodies 'lead' us. Through the mechanism of repression and the formation of the shadow side of our natures (see the entry for Shadow in the Glossary), the emotional body can be in the lead without us being fully aware of it. By placing *too much* emphasis on emotional ventilation, the emotional body can also become the leading aspect. This makes it more, rather than less, difficult for us to leave past hurts behind. It affects the present by producing irrational behaviour patterns and inhibiting the ability to make considered choices. Acting out can become addictive. Too much control can lead to bizarre and dissociated emotional eruptions. A strong energetic connection between root and sacral chakras (as encouraged by Exercise 17, page 143.) brings the necessary balance and interaction between the emotional and feeling bodies.

Romantic and Enduring Love

Let me make it clear that I consider romance to be one of the ingredients of magic. It is, therefore, of great importance among the delights and experiences of life. When there is imbalance, however, in the sacral/heart connection, and between the emotional and feeling bodies, romance can become an obstacle to enduring love.

The stylized illustration of the heart has become a symbol or sign for romantic love. We all hope to enter into the spirit of St Valentine's Day and the reminders it can bring of love's young dream. When used to keep that aspect of love alive within a relationship, it can be very positive.

It is the expectation within the dream of romantic love which can be at fault. Inevitably, in lasting relationships the mundane has to be faced and many relationships have failed because the Prince and his Princess no longer recognize each other behind the frowns over bills or after suffering sleepless nights and dealing with soggy, smelly nappies. We are often conditioned by popular fiction and magazines to expect that romance will continue without us having to work at it. In such cases, when the expectation proves false, the ability to develop enduring love founders.

Another aspect of romantic love which can prevent the growth of the emotional maturity on which enduring love is based is that of possessiveness and jealousy. These emotions cause agonies for the adolescent as first passions and loves develop. Where they exist too strongly in a relationship they are a sign that the link between the emotional and feeling bodies is insufficiently activated. Rather than ensuring constancy of affection, the possessiveness, insecurities, control mechanisms and hurts (real or imagined) which come from jealousy, can drive relationships apart and block the growth of the natural fidelity which is based on mutual respect.

When love is unable to mature, then, once again, the emotional and feeling bodies will usually be out of balance, and Exercise 17 (page 143) can be invaluable when a relationship is going through a difficult patch. When these energetic connections are sound, decisions about the potential in relationships also become clearer. There is less likelihood of 'hanging in there' for the wrong reasons, more strength to weather the mundane, and also, perhaps paradoxically, more likelihood of being able to keep true romance alive despite the obstacles to it.

Twin Souls

Our expectations of love and partnership are also coloured by our desire or drive to find our twin souls. On page 50 Gildas describes the start of the evolutionary journey. The original spark from the Source splits into yin and yang and these become complementary soul threads or stems, each carrying the beads or flowers of potential incarnations.

Gildas goes on to say:

> The longing for the twin soul is well known. When evolution is complete, which means that all the beads on the thread have incarnated and returned, the two strands or stems will become one again. During incarnation, until that is possible, a flower from one stem or a bead from one strand may meet with a flower or bead from its twin essence, but twin souls do not always incarnate at the same time.
>
> The complete being does not incarnate. The flowers from the stems or the beads from the threads are aspects of the essential soul. As many as seven aspects from each stem or strand may be incarnate at any one time and, if they meet, will have a very close relationship. Again, this meeting is rare, since the purpose of incarnation is to gain experience. The impulse behind putting out more than one aspect at a particular period is to ensure as broad a knowledge of that historical earth era as possible. The number of beads on a thread or flowers on a stem varies from soul to soul.
>
> There have been periods in your history where it was more common for twin souls to meet, such as in Atlantean, Egyptian, Grecian or Native American Indian incarnations. In the present time an extraordinary amount of work is often taken on during the course of one incarnation and this means that meeting with twin souls is discouraged by the karmic advisers and helpers. The danger is that the two

beings may be so absorbed in each other that the degree to which they move forward their learning process is lessened. With the dawning of the Golden Age it will be *usual* for twin souls to be working together in incarnation once more. Now, the range of available experience is very great and twin souls must tend to live separately in order to cover as much evolutionary ground as possible.

It may be both disconcerting and disappointing to realize that we are unlikely to meet our perfect mate, or other half, in this present incarnation. Yet, once we know and understand this, a certain discontent and longing in us may be put to rest, as our expectations of the partners we do meet become more realistic. When this particular spiritual perspective is taken, we can see life as an evolutionary workplace and understand more about the overall organization and intent behind the system in which we operate.

The unlikelihood of meeting with our twin souls does not rule out the many possibilities of meeting members of our soul family or wider soul group. These meetings can bring great joy and a great sense of companionship, as well as giving opportunities to be each other's teachers and supporters (see also page 82).

ROOT, SACRAL AND HEART AS A CHAKRA TRIAD

We have so far considered the root/sacral and sacral/heart chakras as separate pairs. Yet these three centres also form an important energetic triad.

Working with the root and sacral chakras helps to stop upsurges of greed and imbalances of power which affect us both personally and collectively. Yet when there is a full, vigorous interaction and balance between the triad now under discussion an important humanizing and tenderizing factor is added. If this particular equilibrium is present, we can rule and shape our microcosmic worlds in a positive way which reflects out into the macrocosm. When the heart link in the triad has yet to be made, we find it harder to throw off conditioning or expectations from the macrocosm, are over-affected by the negativity 'out there', and tend to lose touch with our potential for co-creativity.

Power Games

If the root and sacral pair are insufficiently in communication we tend to get caught up in the playing of power games and the creation of false hierarchies. We can become obsessed with material and worldly power, seemingly blind to any sense of spiritual purpose. Though we may work with the root/sacral pair because we recognize, even minimally, such tendencies within ourselves and want to bring them into harmony as part of our spiritual journey, it is at the collective level that we can see the fullest effects of what can happen when root and sacral are imperfectly connected.

In an era where power, greed and materialism have become false gods, it is important to work with the chakra triad as well as the pairs under discussion. The triadic energy connection complements and enhances the work already done with the pairs. The qualities of touch and tenderness from the heart temper our ability to handle power and to produce good leaders.

Throughout spiritual and religious history, leadership has often been used negatively. The heart dimension frequently gets lost when there is an over-emphasis on dogma and where religious and spiritual practice is based on the enlisting of an elitist few. Belief in a jealous god who breeds fear in would-be followers or devotees is dangerous. Spiritual practice should empower, not disempower and render vulnerable.

Equally, in more worldly terms, leaders who have no true root/sacral/heart triadic connection may be intent on personal gain and power over others. Where there are also imbalances in the relevant single chakras or chakric pairs, only dictatorship – with all its potential for engendering negative anarchy – can result.

When leaders have more of the triadic energy flowing they become more positively and spiritually aligned with the positive potential of leadership for shaping a harmonious world for all. They are more likely to work for the fulfilment of human potential and the empowerment of the individual for the good of the whole. In *The Tao of Leadership* (see Bibliography), John Heider describes the qualities cultivated by leaders with the root/sacral/heart triad in alignment. He says:

The greatest administrators do not achieve production through constraints and limitations. They provide opportunities.

Good leadership consists of motivating people to their highest levels by offering them opportunities, not obligations.

That is how things happen naturally. Life is an opportunity and not an obligation . . .

The group will not prosper if the leader grabs the lion's share of the credit for the good work that has been done.

The group will rebel and resist if the leader relies on strict controls in an effort to make things come out a certain way.

The group members will become deadened and unresponsive if the leader is critical and harsh.

The wise leader is not greedy, selfish, defensive or demanding. That is why the leader can be trusted to allow any event to unfold naturally . . .

Natural events are cyclical, always changing from one extreme toward an opposite . . .

. . . That is the way of nature: to relax what is tense, to fill what is empty, to reduce what is overflowing.

But a society based on materialism and the conquest of nature works to overcome these cycles. If some is good, more must be better and an absolute glut seems best. At the same time, those who have little get even less. By serving others and being generous, the leader knows abundance. By being selfless, the leader helps others realize themselves. By being a disinterested facilitator, unconcerned with praise or pay, the leader becomes potent and successful.

When we are insecure in ourselves we seek aggressive power over others, or become victims, so colluding with patterns of tyranny and oppression. If we seek control of others (because we fear that if they were free they might destroy us) we cannot move to the vision of empowered individuals who mutually empower. If we fear the breakdown of the old order, we can only become prisoners of its structure.

Feelings of insecurity can also make us both greedy and miserly. We stockpile in order to be certain of supplies, but fear to use them in case they should be impossible to replenish. From our greed eventually come waste *and* scarcity, evidenced by such contemporary scandals as the 'butter mountain' and the destruction of surplus harvests in times of glut or abundance, whilst some of our fellow human beings in the Third World are starving.

Lack of self-worth underlies much of the materialistic ethos. Uncertain of our own inner empowerment, we need to make ourselves important or notable by what we possess. Once again, we create waste by discarding the old in order to be in the vanguard of fashion. We become a ravening consumer society by building a calculated obsolescence into that which we manufacture.

Even when we have worked with root/sacral and sacral/heart connections, until the triadic energy is also flourishing we can remain stuck in the pursuit of material objectives. We can lose, or fail to develop, vision or imagination and continue to live in a world where dictatorships, tyrants, victims, and false hierarchies show us to be driven by frustrated and unresolved power and emotional issues. Working with the chakra pairs of this chapter lays down the foundation on which the triadic (root/sacral/heart) connection can be built. The activation of the pairs (root/sacral; sacral/heart) will help us to heal ourselves as individuals, but the healing which permeates out into society does not proceed until an optimum number of us have perceived the different, richer, harmonies which are made possible by activating the root/sacral/heart triad.

When this triad is positively functioning, we become:

– more aware of inner wealth
– more creative in shaping our world
– more discerning in our choice of leaders
– more conscious of the part we, as individuals, may play in creating the poverty or deprivation of others
– more trusting in an abundant universe and therefore more able to link a respect for natural growth patterns and fertility to a true sharing of resources
– more in touch with our self-empowerment and therefore able to be more generous-hearted and empowering towards others
– less motivated by jealousies and envies
– less authoritarian
– less subject to, or enslaved by, swings of fashion.

Diana, Princess of Wales

Much of this book is being written in the aftermath of the sudden death of Diana, Princess of Wales. Reflection on Princess Diana's life and the outcome of her death will bring a deeper understanding of the effect which a person with a strongly functioning root/sacral/heart triad can have on the shaping of collective and individual worlds.

Princess Diana became a popular and compassionate woman who, in addition to her capacity for unconditional love (see also page 243), fully demonstrated in her life the need to link power issues to the heart chakra.

She saw the human being behind each dilemma and the human suffering which continues whilst protocol procrastinates and red tape proliferates. She constantly overcame the divide between the falsely elevated and the ordinary. She knew that she had the human power to make ripples on stagnant ponds and did not shrink from making them. She campaigned for social justice and effectively used her outrage at some aspects of the common human lot.

Despite a tremendous and often desperate struggle, in the face of unmitigating odds, she attained that self-worth which is free from overweening pride and therefore also empowers others to a better vision of self and to hope for the future. Notwithstanding her experience of personal tragedy she maintained an infectious sense of joy, light and healing, which touched, lifted and blessed many, even in the midst of their own harsh encounters with life, sickness, disability, or certain death.

THE ARCHETYPES: CREATIVITY, PEACE, SEXUALITY, POWER AND ABUNDANCE

Creativity

A useful definition of creativity on which to reflect is: 'The coming together of two known but separate forces to produce a new, previously unknown or unmanifest force.'

When we take a spiritual overview of many lifetimes and believe in the interaction of our souls in making incarnational choices, we can see that we do indeed create our own world in the widest sense. Learning to go on co-creating our personal world by linking personality development to the evolution of the soul is a prime objective of spiritual growth. Thus creativity, with its closely connected partner, co-creativity, becomes a driving force by which we live. As such, it is an archetype.

As an archetype, creativity signifies the powerful intercourse between those most basic principles of the universe, yin and yang. Creativity thus incorporates many aspects of sexuality and of our relationships with each other and the universe.

The connections between the root and sacral, and the sacral and heart chakras, are essential to generating spiritual creativity (see Exercise 17, page 143). There is also more about creativity on page 122.

Peace

When there are positive energetic links between the root and sacral, and the sacral and heart chakras, a sense of peace is generated. This background of energetic peace within ourselves can enable us to work out our difficulties even in the emotionally loaded areas of sexuality and violence.

Sometimes we may see peace as a very passive quality, but in reality it is close to harmony which is active and interactive. When a musical note is sounded it reverberates and resonates and causes other notes, with which it is in harmony or relationship, to reverberate back. Peace is a note. When it sounds within us and from us it produces other resonating sounds which positively affect our lives and relationships. The energy balances and movements brought about by practising the exercises on pages 143–7 will help to harmonize your energy system and generate your own personal peace notes. When we sound peace notes in our personal energy fields they reverberate out into the atmosphere, finding and creating resonances in others. When we are considering peace it is particularly true that, if we want to create change around us, we do well to start with ourselves (see Exercise 22, page 149).

Sexuality

A guided journey in a workshop on sexuality and spirituality involved a meeting with the archetype of sexuality. When the archetype was asked to speak, and show some of its many facets, several of the group members had an experience in which the archetype expressed distress at the way in which it had become laden with heavy and negative baggage from humanity. The positive side of the archetype is full of joy, spontaneity, fun, laughter and creativity. It is about celebration of womanhood and manhood and the tremendous potential which exists between the sexes and between the yin/yang principles within each one of us and the universe (see also 'creativity', page 138).

In the area of sexuality we have been given many prohibitions and inhibitions. The dark side of sexuality (rape, sexual abuse, violence, repression and pornography) is very prevalent in our world today. It is very sobering to reflect on what has happened to an archetype which is at the source of the life-force.

As we consider the archetype as an aid to personal healing, we need to look at what we personally have placed upon its shoulders. Seeing what we have to release, and the bright side which the archetype has to offer, can help to shape, activate and direct any healing we need in the areas of sex and sexuality (see Exercise 23, page 150).

Power

Power is an energy. In itself it is neither bad nor good, merely a force to be reckoned with. If we think in terms of 'power to' and 'power of' we are likely to complete the phrase with more positive words and sentiments than if we think in terms of 'power over'. In the spiritual sense we may refer to the 'power to heal', the 'power of healing' or 'the power of prayer'.

Part of the *Chambers' English Dictionary*'s definition of power reads:

> ability to do anything – physical, mental, spiritual, legal,
> etc; capacity for producing an effect; strength; energy; faculty
> of the mind; moving force of anything; right to command;
> authority; rule; influence; control; governing office;
> permission to act; potentiality; strong influence or rule

Power is almost synonymous with life-force. Without it, life goes into stasis. It is an energy which powers the creation and continuity of the universe and at the same time a force which can be used for physical, mental, emotional or spiritual destruction. It is an intensity within us which demands that we come to terms with it. Without power we cannot function. If it is wrongly distributed or managed it can lead to great suffering. The power of the Divine is 'aweful'; the consequences of temporal power can be both 'aweful' *and* 'awful'!

As an archetype, power includes authority and leadership. Our personal power or empowerment is affected by our interaction with, and our relationship to, these factors of society.

Power is often automatically seen as something rigid, negative or destructive. This interpretation of the archetype says much about our frequent inability to come to terms with it. Religious and spiritual teachings tend to leave us confused about our inner power/divinity by facing us with unresolved and paradoxical questions: 'Are we created in the image of God, maintaining an essence or spark of the Divine within? or 'Are we outcast, miserable sinners, unworthy of the Divine, and with the inner spark either non-existent or extinguished by our misdemeanours?'

Contemplating power as an archetype means being aware of its potential for misuse and yet also learning to come to terms with it as a pure and vital force of divine origin. It means learning to use this force for inner change and attaining the belief that all obstacles can be either overcome or transformed.

Abundance

We can see abundance as an archetype only if we hold the belief that it is a Divine Principle. Religious teachings, together with spiritual paths and disciplines, have tended to lead us to regard self-deprivation and the practice of abstinence as virtues. Hedonism is often seen as the ultimate obstacle to spirituality. Paradoxically, religious thinkers have sometimes seen the rich man as divinely blessed or favoured and the poor man as having smaller hope of, or right to, divine favour. Though the hymn 'All Things Bright and Beautiful' has been many people's favourite, and speaks of abundance, it used to contain the controversial verse:

> The rich man in his castle,
> The poor man at his gate,
> The Lord God made them all
> And ordered their estate.

Perhaps another lesson which Diana, Princess of Wales, had to teach us, was that of living abundantly. Worldly wealth apart, she threw herself into life and drew an abundance of experience towards her. By so-doing she rendered herself vulnerable. She even suffered from, but overcame, anorexia and bulimia, those disorders of our times which symbolically say so much about our abundance/scarcity confusions.

Fear of life, and fear of scarcity, create not only greed, but transgressions against the archetype of abundance. We tend to believe that things are rationed and will run out; then transfer this belief to things emotional – particularly love. In this way we become comparative and competitive. 'Who do you love best?', 'Who do you love most?', 'Do you love me as much as him?', are questions many of us ask of parents during childhood, or of lovers during adolescence. It seems that we go on asking those questions of gods, goddesses or the universe, for most of our lives.

We tend to divide people around us into those we love and those we don't. Of course there will always be natural affinities and attractions (see page 132) but over-quantifying and thinking in polarities makes it difficult for us to get to that place of feeling and acceptance where we cherish the whole underlying essence of humanity and are both moved and inspired by the human condition. Before we can truly open to abundance we must recognize that we, personally, are cherishable and that the universe has the potential to cherish us.

There is nothing wrong with material abundance and we do not have to misuse resources in order to create it. In every field of our endeavours it is not what we possess which is wrong, but our attitude to it. Non-attachment, an oft-quoted and oft-misinterpreted key word for the spiritual path, does not mean that we cannot possess – only that we should not hoard and use possessions as a means of acquiring power. Abundance is a flow. *Over-attachment* to what we possess creates unlawful dams in the river. If we wish to create material abundance in our lives and release hang-ups about money we must come to terms with the archetype of abundance and see ourselves as worthy of, and having full permission to, receive and possess.

Being taught to hold something back and never to go 'over the top' are contradictions to, and denials of, abundance as an archetype. Setting norms puts those who do not conform 'beyond the fringe' and can be a denial of creativity (which is closely related to, and inspired by, abundance). If we can create and therefore live creatively, abundance will never fail. Linking the root, sacral and heart chakra triad will help us identify any personal blockages, insecurities and 'hang-ups' which may be preventing the manifestation of abundance in our lives. It will also activate and heal energy patterns within us which attract the abundance flow.

EXERCISES

Exercise 17
Connecting the Sacral and Root Chakras

For this exercise you should sit or stand with your spine straight and supported if necessary. Your legs should be uncrossed, unless sitting in a full cross-legged, semi-lotus or lotus position.

- Begin with central column breathing (see page 17).
- When you feel centred, let your breathing rhythm help you to focus your attention into your sacral chakra. Breathe in and out through your sacral chakra, taking the breath in through the petals and breathing it out through the stem. You can either concentrate solely on the breath rhythm or, if you wish, you can also visualize an amber or orange colour, thus combining two exercises for activating your sacral chakra (see page 156 for more description and explanation of these colours).
- After five to ten in/out breaths through your sacral chakra, change the pattern by breathing into the centre of the chakra, holding the breath for a count of three, and then breathing down into your root chakra and out deeply into the earth for a further five to ten in/out breaths. (If using colour visualization at the same time, you should still be working with amber or orange.)
- If you are using colour as well as breath, change the colour now to either a deep rosy red, or to mauve (see page 41). Breathe up from the earth into the centre of your root chakra, hold the breath there for a count of three, then breathe up into the centre of your sacral chakra and out through its petals (five to ten in/out breaths).
- Finish this linking exercise by using again the sacral–root–earth breath sequence described above (last step but one).

Exercise 18
Correcting the Downward Energy Spiral

Sit or stand with your spine straight for this exercise (as for Exercise 17, above).

- Begin with central column breathing (see page 17).
- When you feel centred, breathe in and out through the

petals of your sacral chakra. Visualize a spiral of energy
which flows down from the centre of your sacral chakra
through the downward-pointing petals of your root
chakra and into the earth. (*When this spiral is out of balance,
as described on pages 171–72, the energy dissipates, either in the
root chakra itself, or as it reaches the earth, without becoming
engaged in an essential, complementary, upward flow.*) To
correct or strengthen the complementary flow, imagine a
huge diamond lying deep within the earth. Visualize the
downward energy spiral from the sacral chakra going
deeply and strongly down through the earth into this
diamond crystal. Use your breath to help you to breathe
the spiral strongly downwards and into the diamond (five
to ten in/out breaths).

- Now visualize a strong upward-flowing energy spiral,
  coming from the diamond crystal in the earth, up through
  your root chakra, through your sacral chakra, on up via the
  central column, through your solar plexus chakra, to
  the centre of your heart chakra. Assist this energy spiral on
  its journey by breathing it up. When it reaches the centre
  of your heart chakra breathe it out through the petals of
  your heart, keeping the sense of the spiral strongly in
  mind (five to ten in/out breaths).

This exercise is similar to the central column breathing
described in Exercise 1 (page 17). But here the emphasis is
on correcting the energy spiral so that there are no power
loop backs between the sacral and root chakras (see also
page 171).

Exercise 19
Connecting the Sacral and Heart Chakras

Position yourself as for Exercise 17 (see page 143).

- Begin with central column breathing (see page 17).
- Breathe in through the petals of your sacral chakra and out through its stem. If you wish to visualize colour at the same time as focusing on the breath, use amber or gold (see page 156) (five to ten in/out breath sequences).
- Breathe in through the petals of your sacral chakra (still using amber or gold if you wish). Hold the breath in the centre of the sacral chakra to a count of three, then breathe up through the central column into the centre of your heart chakra, and out through the petals of your heart (five to ten in/out breath sequences).
- Breathe in through the petals of your heart and out through its stem. If you wish to use colour at the same time work with spring green (see page 101) (five to ten in/out breath sequences).
- Breathe in through the petals of your heart chakra, still using the spring green visualization if you wish. Hold the breath in the centre of the heart for a count of three. Breathe down through the central column into the centre of your sacral chakra and out through its petals (five to ten in/out breath sequences).

Exercise 20
Connecting the Root/Sacral/Heart triad

Position yourself as for Exercise 17 (see page 143).

- Begin with central column breathing (see page 17).
- When you feel centred, begin to breathe in and out

through the petals of your heart chakra (five to ten in/
out breath sequences).

- Now breathe in to the centre of your heart chakra, hold
  your breath for a count of three, and then breathe down
  through the central column into the centre of your sacral
  chakra. Breathe out through the petals of your sacral
  chakra (five to ten in/out breath sequences).
- Breathe in through the petals of your sacral chakra, hold
  the breath in the centre of your sacral chakra for a count
  of three, and then breathe down into the centre of your
  root chakra and out through its petals into the earth (five
  to ten in/out breath sequences).
- Breathe in through the petals of your root chakra, hold
  the breath in its centre for a count of three, breathe up
  through your central column into your heart chakra and
  out through the petals of your heart (five to ten in/out
  breath sequences).
- Now take a deep breath in through the petals of your heart
  chakra, visualizing it as an energy stream which travels out
  through the stem of your heart chakra, down your spine
  and in through the stem of your sacral chakra to its
  centre, and then down, through your central column to
  your root chakra, and out into the earth (five to ten in/
  out breath sequences).
- Breathe in through the downward-facing petals of your root
  chakra, and visualize your breath as a stream of energy
  which comes into the centre of your sacral chakra, out
  through its stem, up your spine, in through the stem of
  your heart and out through your heart chakra petals (five
  to ten in/out breath sequences).
- Conclude this exercise with central column breathing for
  a further five to ten in/out breath sequences.

Exercise 21
Guided Visualization for Contacting the Archetype of Creativity

Making sure that you will be undisturbed and that you have paper, writing and drawing materials to hand, sit or lie down in a comfortable position, with a blanket for warmth if necessary. Your body should be symmetrically arranged and your legs should not be crossed at the knees or ankles.

- Begin with central column breathing (see page 17). When you feel centred, let your breath rhythm help you to focus on, and thus activate, your root chakra and your sacral chakra.
- Now bring the breath rhythm into your heart chakra so that each in-breath and out-breath activates your heart energy . . . Travel on the heart breath into your inner world or landscape and find yourself in a meadow . . . As you experience your meadow, activate all your inner senses so that you see the objects and colours . . . hear the sounds . . . touch the textures . . . smell the fragrances . . . and taste the tastes . . .
- As you look out into the landscape from your meadow, you can see a beautiful rainbow . . . The spot where the rainbow begins (or ends), rising up powerfully from the earth, is very clear . . . You know that in your inner world you can do that which is improbable in the outer . . . You can travel to the spot where the rainbow has its source . . . When you arrive at this magical place the colours are very clear . . . They are so tangible as to be almost touchable . . . They seem to have a fragrance and a sound . . . Within this rainbow of light, if you invite it to do so, the archetype of creativity will appear, and as you watch, will blend these wondrous colours for your entertainment . . . They will be mixed, matched, blended, until new colours of every shade,

depth and texture appear for you . . . Note how two known colours, blended together in different ways, can produce new colour ranges and tones . . . In observing this, you are observing the basic interaction of the force which is creativity . . .

- As you watch, if you have any pressing life problem or question which needs an answer or solution, become aware of it and ask that it may receive a blessing from the archetype of creativity . . . If there is no particular problem you want to bring here, then ask that your own inner creativity be blessed and inspired . . .
- When you have been with the archetype of creativity for not more than fifteen minutes, thank the archetype for its presence, and leave the rainbow source . . . Come back to the meadow where you began this visualization . . . Gradually become aware of the rhythm of your breathing in your heart centre . . . Feel your body in touch with your chair or the floor . . . Come fully back into the outer world . . . Visualize a cloak of light with a hood right around you . . .
- Take time to draw and record your journey.

Exercise 22
Reflection for Contacting the Archetype of Peace

Making sure that you will be undisturbed, sit or lie in a comfortable position, with your body symmetrically arranged. Unless sitting in a cross-legged or lotus posture do not cross your legs at the knees or ankles. Support your spine if necessary and have a rug for warmth if you wish.

- Begin with central column breathing (see page 17).
- When you feel centred, breathe in through the petals of your sacral chakra, into its centre, and then down through

the root chakra and out into the earth . . . (five to ten in/out breath sequences).

- Now breathe in through the petals of your heart chakra, into its centre and then down through the central column, through the centre of the sacral chakra, through the root and out into the earth . . . (five to ten in/out breath sequences).

- Continue breathing from your heart chakra down into the earth and begin to recite, mentally, the mantram 'At peace', repeating the two words over and over again, and letting any thoughts or images which come to you during this process pass by as though on a television screen in front of you, so that you are noting them without engaging with them . . . (ten to fifteen minutes).

- Visualize a cloak of light with a hood around you and then write down or draw any impressions about peace which came to you during this reflection.

Exercise 23
Guided Visualization for Contacting the Archetype of Sexuality

There are two possible stages in this visualization. The first takes you to the archetype of sexuality in its most positive form. The second gives you the opportunity to ask the archetype to show you any negativity it is carrying for you. You can do both parts of the visualization on the same occasion if you wish, separate them by a period of time or, if your sexuality needs a lot of healing, make sure you only do the second part when you are completely ready or can be supported by a trusted friend, partner or counsellor.

Making sure that you will be undisturbed, and that you have paper, writing and drawing materials to hand, sit or lie down in a comfortable position, with a blanket for warmth if necessary. Your body should be symmetrically arranged and, unless sitting in a cross-legged or lotus position, your legs should not be crossed at the knees or ankles.

- Begin with central column breathing (see page 17). When you feel centred, let your breath rhythm help you to focus on, and thus activate, your root chakra and your sacral chakra.
- Now bring the breath rhythm into your heart chakra so that each in-breath and out-breath activates your heart energy . . . Travel on the heart breath into your inner world or landscape and find yourself in a meadow . . . As you experience your meadow, activate all your inner senses so that you see the objects and colours . . . hear the sounds . . . touch the textures . . . smell the fragrances . . . and taste the tastes . . .
- Find a quiet, sunny spot in the meadow where you can sit and reflect for a while . . . It is good to sit with your back against a tree or a rock . . . As you reflect, in preparation for your journey to meet the archetype of sexuality, consider any questions you would like to ask and be aware of any aspects of your sexuality which need healing . . . (five minutes).
- From the meadow you can view your landscape. . . Begin now to look around and as you do so, express the wish to meet with the archetype of sexuality. . . Somewhere on higher ground in your landscape you can see an area of light and you know that this is the place where you can meet safely with the archetype. . . In the next three minutes travel to this place of light and once again find somewhere where you can sit comfortably and ask the archetype to appear. . . Remember that you are meeting the clear archetype of sexuality, in its most positive form. . .

The two stages for working with the archetype are now given. You may wish to read again the suggestions given above, at the start of this exercise.

Stage 1

- When the archetype appears to you, ask it any question you have or tell it about any healing you need for your sexuality . . . The archetype may speak to you, you may get an inner knowing, or you may see a symbol or be given a symbolic gift . . . (five to ten minutes).

If you are not proceeding to Stage 2, return now to your meadow, to your awareness of your breathing and of your body in contact with the chair or floor. Put a cloak of light with a hood around you and take time to draw and record your journey.

Stage 2

- You may now ask the archetype of sexuality to show you anything of a more negative nature which it is carrying for you and ask it for help in releasing any fears, inhibitions or negative beliefs which may prevent you from owning your true sexual nature and orientation . . . (five minutes).
- Ask the archetype of sexuality how you can help to relieve it, and yourself, of these particular burdens . . . Again, you may inwardly hear the archetype speak, experience an inner knowing, see a symbol, or be given a symbolic gift . . . (five minutes).
- Knowing that, once you have used an area of your inner landscape, you can always return, thank and take leave of the archetype of sexuality, and return to your meadow . . . From your meadow become aware of your breathing and of your body in contact with the chair or floor . . . Visualize a cloak of light with a hood right around you . . . Come fully back into the outer world and take time to draw and record your journey.

Exercise 24
Reflection on Your Connection with the Archetype of Power

Making sure that you will be undisturbed and with paper, drawing and writing materials to hand, sit or lie down in a comfortable position, with your spine straight, your body symmetrical and your legs uncrossed at the knees or ankles. Have a rug for warmth if you wish.

- Begin with central column breathing (see page 17).
- When you feel centred, begin to write a letter to the archetype of power. Make the theme of this letter a review of your life, starting from the present and going back as far as you wish, in seven-year stages, recalling all the life events which have affected your relationship with power.
- You might begin, for instance, with today's date and then:

  Dear Archetype of Power,
  At the present moment I feel in charge of my life in the following areas . . .
  I feel less in charge when I am put into a difficult position by . . .
  Seven years ago, the things in my life connected with power were . . .
  Seven years before that you were helping me to . . .

- Go back to around the time of your birth if you can. Although you will not remember this time, you will have been told things about your birth and the circumstances in which it took place. Reflect on, and write or draw about the balance of power in the family at the time that you were born.
- If you do not wish to write in full, you can make key word notes of your life-review or make a series of drawings.

- If you do not want to do your whole life at one sitting, you can spread this exercise over a period of time.

Exercise 25
Inner Abundance (A Guided Journey)

Making sure that you will be undisturbed and with pens, drawing materials and paper to hand, sit or lie down in a comfortable position with your spine straight, your body symmetrically arranged and, unless sitting in a cross-legged or lotus position, have your legs uncrossed at the knees or ankles. Have a rug for warmth if you wish.

- Begin with central column breathing (see page 17).
- When you feel centred, begin to breathe in and out through the petals of your heart chakra ... Travel on your heart breath, into your inner landscape and find yourself in a meadow ...
- Take the opportunity of being in the meadow, to activate your inner senses ... See the objects and the colours ... Hear the sounds ... Small the fragrances ... Touch the textures ... Taste the tastes ...
- You are going to take an overview of your inner landscape and you can choose how you wish accomplish this:
  - You might travel to a high point in your landscape.
  - You might fly on a magic carpet, which you can call to you and which is totally in your control.
  - You might ride on a horse, a unicorn, a winged horse or winged unicorn, on a large bird, or on the back of some other inner animal.
  - You might ascend on a rainbow, a single colour, a sunbeam or moonbeam.
  - You might fly, hand in hand, with an inner wise figure, guardian or angel.
- You may make a conscious choice of your mode of

transport, or it may appear naturally, in your visualization . . . When you are ready to travel, set out to survey your landscape, taking the key word 'Abundance' with you . . .

- As you travel, become aware of all the areas of your landscape which are lush, fruitful and beautiful . . . Anything representing abundance can be present in your landscape:
  - Fields of ripe corn
  - Orchards full of blossoms or fruits
  - Full-flowing rivers or waterfalls
  - Lush water meadows
  - Tree-covered mountain slopes with alpine meadows, where cows graze
  - Blue seas, with sandy shores
  - Beautiful lakes
  - Thick, fertile forests
  - Places warmed but not burned by the sun
  - Areas abundant with flowers
  - Crystal and jewelled caves
  - Gold or silver mines, well looked after and not blotting the landscape
  - Places of abundant peace
  - Ever-burning, but non-consuming, fires or flames
  - Deep, fish-filled oceans
  - Places of abundant wildlife

  These are suggestions, you may find any or all of these or other different areas which represent abundance for you . . .
- Take about ten minutes for this overview of your inner abundance and then return to your meadow . . .
- Spend a few moments in your meadow, before you return to the outer world, to reflect on the abundance within, its distribution and the ease with which you found it . . .
- Ask yourself how you feel about this inner abundance . . .
- Thank any companions you had for this journey, return from your meadow, to the consciousness of your breathing

in your heart centre . . . your awareness of your body and your outer surroundings . . . Visualize a cloak of light, with a hood of light right around you . . .

- Take time to draw or record your journey and to reflect on anything it may teach you about your inner relationship with abundance.

THE COLOURS

The colours for the sacral chakra are: orange, amber and gold (non-metallic). They are colours of vitality.

Positively, orange is warming and energizing. To some people, in its more vivid forms it can be experienced as enervating or confrontational. If this is your personal reaction to orange, focus more on amber and gold shades.

When convalescing from illness, feeling tired or just needing an energy boost, visualizing orange light flowing into your sacral chakra will be effective. A bowl of oranges in a room, or some orange or amber glass hanging in a window where sunlight can pass through it also helps general vitality and the development of the sacral chakra.

Negative tones of orange are disharmonizing and can generate unrest or even violence.

Amber is a colour which we use in everyday life to indicate caution – or proceed with caution. In other words it is used to remind us to be aware. One of the most basic and effective spiritual lessons is to learn to 'be present' at all times and in all situations. Being present also helps us protect ourselves from the unexpected or negative sides of life. When our presence is finely attuned we automatically pre-empt situations. We are 'on the ball' and can therefore prepare ourselves for action, whether it be for avoidance, confrontation or participation.

On the negative side, amber may make us over-cautious or generate non-specific fears and anxieties.

Non-metallic gold is a warm, glowing colour which generates creativity, especially in human relationships.

Negative or murky tones of gold can cause depression or lethargy.

Use these colours as suggested in Exercise 8 (page 42) to develop, awaken and heal your sacral chakra.

The colours for the root chakra are red, brown and mauve; and, for the heart chakra, spring green, rose and rose amethyst. To strengthen the colours in your root and heart chakras, refer to Exercise 8 (page 42).

THE FRAGRANCES

Musk and amber stimulate the sacral centre, while rosemary and rose-geranium quieten it. Musk oil is a plant product, as is amber, and these fragrances should not be confused with the animal extracts often used in the perfume industry. Use the stimulating fragrances if you have a tendency to be rather passive, lacking in vitality, have difficulty in making choices or need more sexual vitality. Use the quietening fragrances if you are over-active, fear loss of control or find it difficult to 'play', relax or sleep.

For the root chakra the quietening fragrances are cedarwood and patchouli, and the stimulating ones are musk, lavender and hyacinth. For the heart chakra the quietening fragrances are sandalwood and rose, and the stimulating ones are pine and honeysuckle. See page 43 for suggestions for using the fragrances.

You can experiment with blending fragrances for the sacral/ root and sacral/heart connections.

THE CRYSTALS

Refer to page 44 and the Glossary for general guidance on using crystals. The crystals which will best help the issues considered in this chapter are:

Agate To strengthen your relationship to life and bring a *joie de vivre*. It encourages abundance and helps to heal fears of, or wounds from, poverty and deprivation. It balances inner masculine and feminine energies. It helps us to be good parents to our children.

Aventurine To help release blocked creativity and activate the imagination.

Jasper This is a stone of power and empowerment. The water element is often interpreted as being unstable and over-sensitive but it can also be directed, active and full of power. Jasper encourages the blossoming of these latter qualities without loss of sensitivity.

Chrysoberyl This is a beautiful stone, having many different colours and forms, of which emerald is one. Chrysoberyls are comparatively rare and expensive but they attract and produce kindness and generosity. They revitalize all our energies and are sometimes called the 'stone of perpetual youth'.

Angelite A stone which, as its name suggests, helps to attract angelic blessings. It is a transformative stone which helps lift the burden of old patterns and blockages from us.

PRAYERS OR AFFIRMATIONS

The root chakra prayer or affirmation is:

Through incarnation may spirit be brought into matter.
Through rootedness may life-force be recharged and
exchanged. We acknowledge wholeness and seek to gain
and to reflect acceptance.

The sacral chakra prayer or affirmation is:

> May the unity of humanity with each other and the earth
> enable true creativity. May release from a sense of sin and
> unworthiness lead us into the full knowledge of our
> empowerment as co-creators, at one with, and a part of
> the Divine.

The heart chakra prayer or affirmation is:

> In the golden centre of the rose of the heart may tender
> compassion be linked to unconditional love. May true
> detachment enable growth and continuity. Through the
> understanding of birth within death and death within
> birth may there be transformation.

For suggestions on using prayers or affirmations, see page 45.

Chapter 7

Song of Myself:
The Individual in the World

Key Issues: The Jigsaw Puzzle of Self, Work and Expression in the World; Being Heard and Finding Your Voice

Chakra Pairs: Sacral and Solar Plexus; Sacral and Throat

Archetype: The World

This chapter will help you to:
- gain greater insight into the many aspects of your personality
- better understand the power of self-expression and gain easier access to it

---

AREAS OF INFLUENCE

For a list of the areas of influence for the sacral chakra see page 117.

The Solar Plexus Chakra

Location Just below the sternum, extending down to the navel (stem in corresponding position at the back)

Key Words Logic, Reason, Opinion, Assimilation, Psychic Intuition

Developmental Age 8–12 years

Colours Yellow, Gold, Rose

Element Fire

Sense Sight

Body Astral

Glandular Connection Adrenals

Quietening Fragrances Vetivert, Rose

Stimulating Fragrances Bergamot, Ylang-ylang

Crystals and Gemstones Yellow Citrine, Apatite, Calcite, Kunzite, Rose Quartz, Iron Pyrites (Fool's Gold), Topaz, Malachite

Prayer or Affirmation

Through the gift of fire, let reason, logic, opinion and assimilation become truly linked to inspiration that we are not bound within limitation and separation.

The Throat Chakra

Location The neck (petals at the front, stem at the back)

Key Words Expression, Responsibility, Communication, Universal Truth

Developmental Age 15–21 years

Colours Blue, Silver, Turquoise

Element Ether/Akasha

Sense Hearing

Body Mental

Glandular Connection Thyroid and Parathyroids

Quietening Fragrances Lavender, Hyacinth

Stimulating Fragrances Patchouli, White Musk

Crystals and Gemstones Lapis Lazuli, Aquamarine, Sodalite, Turquoise, Sapphire

Prayer or Affirmation

Help us to develop responsibility. May universal truth impregnate causal action so that the voice of humanity may find true harmony with the voice of the earth.

THE SACRAL AND SOLAR PLEXUS AS A CHAKRA PAIR

The solar plexus is a complex centre, as can be seen from the range of its key words. Perhaps most of its complexity comes from its connection to our lower will, personality and ego. When we are looking at living more spiritually and bringing meaning to life, the lower self or ego has to feel recognized and respected, before it can begin to cooperate with higher destiny.

Personality and Ego

There is a traditional spiritual injunction which instructs the follower of the path to 'lose the ego'. This is often wrongly understood and quoted out of context. My feeling is that it has even been mistranslated. Those three words, standing alone, as a key to spirituality, are suspect and dangerous and do not allow for the bridge which needs to be made between the psychological and the spiritual worlds.

Our ego is our identity. It must be strongly built before any wider explorations can take place with safety. Some psychotic conditions are linked to loss of identity. There are far too many instances of spiritual and religious travellers becoming lost and needing psychiatric treatment, simply because their ego structure was not strong enough for the intensity of the spiritual journey which they had undertaken.

Spirituality cannot *replace* psychological growth, without spirituality, does not necessarily answer all our questions. But when the two go hand in hand, human potential soars beyond expectations. Eventually, and perhaps somewhat paradoxically in view of the foregoing, the attainment of spiritual goals is dependent upon the *surrender* of the ego, with grace and joy, to the higher will and purpose. If that which is surrendered is a strong and well-honed tool, then it will potentially be a better instrument for that higher will.

The solar plexus, then, focuses us on personality development. Yet at the same time, with fire as its element, it is the seat of vision. When the solar plexus is functioning healthily our physical as well as our spiritual sight can improve. The question which the solar plexus prompts us to ask is: 'How do I see the world and how does the world see me?'.

Logic, Reason and Opinion

The key words of logic, reason and opinion belong strongly to the aspect of the solar plexus which is connected with our personality and our ability to manage the mundane well. In life we need a logical and reasonable approach. We need to be able to form and state personal opinions. An independent rationality is needed in order to make decisions about life which allow us to reach our personal and full potential. Intellect and mind have an important relationship with the solar plexus. The sacral centre and its connections to root and heart are concerned with empowerment, as we saw in Chapter 6. The solar plexus has its own input into a continued empowerment process. It is not possible to form and affirm our personal belief systems or to challenge any of society's without the qualities of logic, reason and opinion.

The Psychic Faculty

Though the solar plexus might be called the 'seat' of the lower will, with its connection to the sense of vision and to qualities of psychic intuition, it is also a centre of awareness of other worlds and the recognition that there is more than one reality.

Many people who come to esoteric spiritual study are confused by the difference between the psychic, the spiritual and the use of the word 'psyche' in psychology and psychotherapy.

Psychologically speaking, 'psychic' refers to that which is 'of the psyche' (see Glossary). It is used to describe the interacting personality and behaviour patterns which make each individual a unique and multi-faceted being.

In esoteric realms the word 'psychic' is used to denote a particular kind of sensitivity. The psychic individual may have premonitions, either in dreams or through 'hunches' or 'knowings'. Crystal ball gazers use the psychic faculty. Tarot card, palm and astrology readings are re-establishing themselves now as serious studies offering valuable spiritual guidance. They can also be practised specifically and solely from a psychic level.

The psychic faculty is an important ingredient in spiritual growth and practice. But it must be taken further and connected to the higher centres in the chakra system if it is to relate to more than our material world, the future, our love lives, 'luck' and all the areas generally associated with 'fortune-telling'.

Some people become so over-fascinated by phenomena linked to psychic energy that their pursuit of evidence of telekinesis, spoon-bending, clock-stopping, poltergeist hauntings and psychometry can become a serious obstacle on their spiritual path. Others, confusing the psychic with darker occult practices, become very afraid and often retreat behind the strong boundaries of a dogmatic and literal religion.

Indeed the psychic world can be both over-fascinating and very frightening, but psychic energy is a necessary ingredient in the vision and power which enable us to see, define, implement and change our spiritual direction where necessary.

The Element of Fire

Fire consumes but also sets processes in motion, changes things and enables assimilation. We may refer to ourselves as burning with desire, passion or purpose. Or we may say we are *fired* by imagination or the spirit.

When the solar plexus is under-functioning we tend to get stuck on an inappropriate treadmill, unable to see how to bring about creative change in our lives. Vision, as well as action, can be blocked. An active fire element, nourished by a well-functioning solar plexus, brings enjoyment and passion into our lives.

An over-active solar plexus or fire element can make us over-fiery, dry-skinned, irritable, uncomfortable, and prickly to ourselves and others. In our bodies food may be burned up too quickly and nutrients imperfectly absorbed.

Sub-Personalities

The solar plexus chakra is connected to the development and expression of the lower will and the personality or ego self. It needs the dynamic animation and attributes which come from the sacral centre in order to feed the development of this most basic part of ourselves. As we come to terms with our internal drives and conditioning, so the sacral and solar plexus chakras work powerfully together.

As the sacral energy blends with that of the solar plexus, we are led to the basic question: 'What/who do I mean when I say "I"?' In asking this, we become aware of our complexity and multiplicity. Somewhere there is a central integrating 'I', but it can seem elusive as we observe that 'a part of me feels this . . . but another part feels that . . .'. In matters of choice, how do we finally arrive at what 'I' as a central being wants, or become able to make a creative compromise which allows scope for all the rich, contributing parts?

These are the dilemmas of life. They underlie not only the search for 'I' in a psychological and worldly sense, but also the drive to search for spiritual meaning and purpose. Both the dilemma and the solution are contained within the maturation process of the sacral/solar plexus link. Exercise 26 (on page 175) is a balancing and connecting exercise for the sacral/solar plexus chakras. Basic integrative psychological work is supported when the energy connection is made, and the energy connection becomes stronger when the psychological work goes alongside.

The concept of the higher self and the 'beads on the thread' (see page 50) may lead us to suppose that the higher self is in charge and is the integrating force which we seek. Yet the being which we are on earth, the personality from which we function, fully exists in its own right. If we are too anxious to let the higher self take over, we may give insufficient importance to ego development. The tool which the higher self would use is then insufficiently formed and could be subject to delusions of grandeur, inability to make choices, slavishness to authority, a sense of non-being, or psychosis. These are the dangers which can exist when psychological understanding and spiritual growth become divorced from each other.

When we are psychologically aware of our many parts and work to understand them, we come to a place of integration in which we appreciate our own richness and multi-faceted potential. The voice which says 'I' is informed by that potential and has a wisdom and maturity of its own. If it then chooses to link with a higher self and pursue a deeper meaning and purpose in life, a state called 'Individuation' by Jung and 'Self-Actualization' by Maslow is attained (see C.G. Jung in the Bibliography).

The Italian psychologist, Assagioli, who formulated the system of self-analysis known as psychosynthesis (see Pierro Ferrucci in the Bibliography), spoke of the many facets within ourselves as sub-personalities. Earlier, Jung had spoken of the persona or mask. Our working selves are usually very different from our relaxed, private or holiday selves. We, and those with whom we live and work, need these masks, which help us to play the many different roles life demands of us. We even wear certain uniforms to help the persona to operate: the pin-striped suit for business, the apron for housework, the sporting gear for jogging, the T-shirt for relaxation, the formal or beautiful clothes for entertaining and party-going, are all supports for essential aspects of our day-to-day interactions.

The concept of the sub-personality goes further than that of the persona and refers to the deeper dynamics at work within the psyche. We use the persona more consciously. The sub-personalities develop as a result of conditioning and can be survival mechanisms. They are distinctive energies within the psyche. Ferrucci, a disciple of Assagioli, refers to them as 'degraded archetypes'.

Conditioning influences often derive from degraded or mis-interpreted archetypal forces. In order to deal with the growth difficulties inflicted in this way, we ingest or inwardly create the degraded archetypes which are our sub-personalities. They usually manifest as pairs of opposites.

People who have been required to be over-orderly in child-hood will probably have an obsessively tidy sub-personality but also one which is disordered and chaotic. People who have been subject to power and manipulation may have an inner tyrant but also an inner victim. People who have been required to be too 'good' may have an inner 'goody-goody' but also a naughty, devious, dishonest or sly sub-personality.

These polarized pairs perpetuate each other. We push away those parts of ourselves which we consider to be undesirable. Our success at this means that, until we begin to work with them, sub-personalities are relatively unconscious. Things which exist but are denied gain autonomy. Thus, autonomous sub-personalities may emerge to surprise and embarrass us in unexpected situations, particularly when we are under stress. The remark from friends 'I've never seen that side of you before', or your own self-criticism: 'I really don't know what got into me', are usually warnings that an autonomous or somewhat dissociated sub-personality has revealed itself.

Sub-personalities are rewarding to work with. They reveal themselves readily when we seek them out, telling their stories and helping us to understand what they seek and why they have developed. They will eventually become important allies on our journey to self-knowledge and integration. Knowing and working with them will eventually make our connection with our higher selves clearer and more productive.

Exercise 28 on page 177 will help you to get in touch with your sub-personalities. Use it alongside exercise linking the sacral and solar plexus energies on page 175.

THE SACRAL AND THROAT AS A CHAKRA PAIR

After the crown/root connection (see Chapter 2) that between sacral and throat is the strongest natural link within the chakra system. Weaknesses in this interaction can seriously affect our life and health, while strengthening the connection can help us to function more strongly in the world.

Since the sevenfold chakra system is sub-divided into two interacting groups and the throat chakra is a member of each, it is a gateway chakra. As one of the five lower chakras, it is related to an element, a developmental age and a sense. As the first of three upper chakras, it is concerned with transpersonal expression and connections to the higher self, spirit and soul.

The throat chakra is connected to the sense of hearing, but also to the voice. The question to ask at the throat chakra is: 'How do I hear the world and how does the world hear me?'

How we hear ourselves and how we 'sound ourselves' is also important. As always, the sense for this chakra needs to be interpreted symbolically as well as actually. When a note is sounded, it resonates and reverberates, attracting answering sounds in various harmonic forms or disharmonies. When we strike our true note, disharmonies are reduced and we draw positive synchronicities and compatibilities towards us. Thus life will flow more smoothly because we will recognize that we are always in the right place at the right time. If we have felt lonely in life, and our family of origin has been largely of genetic rather than spiritual derivation, learning to sound our true note attracts friends, companions and family from our soul group towards us and helps to heal our roots (see also Chapter 4).

Strengthening the throat chakra and its connections helps us to find our own note and to sound it with confidence.

The connection to voice and hearing means that the throat chakra is concerned with the actual and metaphoric aspects of finding one's voice and being heard – or the way in which one expresses oneself in the world. At a more spiritual level the throat enables us to connect to our higher selves and our spiritual qualities. Once this link is made, we become uncompromising in expressing our true selves.

During the developmental age of the throat chakra (15–21 years), we go through the rite of passage of 'coming of age', when we are legally adult and therefore held totally responsible for all our actions.

Spiritual coming of age is concerned with responding to, and interpreting the requirements of, a divine or higher purpose. Working with the throat chakra helps us to know and respond to our calling or vocation in life.

Communication

Communication is a complex subject. We develop language in order to communicate with each other, yet what we communicate goes far beyond the written word or the power of speech and hearing. Body language, the clothes we wear, the subtle smells we exude, and what is left unsaid as well as what is said, are all important factors.

Our bodies work for us because our organs are in communication with each other. Each body part is dependent upon another, though we may only become aware of the existence of this interdependent communication when there is a minor or major breakdown within the system. When our diet agrees with us, our digestive and eliminative processes work happily together and we do not need to think about them. But if we eat something disagreeable the system lets us know about it. If we develop a serious bout of flu we can no longer get our limbs to obey us. The internal communication knows that rest is required. In times of health and well-being the signallings of our miraculous and finely tuned inner communication system remain unconscious and are taken for granted. Working with the throat chakra enables us to listen better to our bodies and become more attuned to our health patterns.

With much communication linked to sound, it is interesting that some scientists believe that sound is the basic pattern which enabled the universe to come into being. When we strive to understand higher abstract laws, we have to name them and speak them before they truly come into being or manifestation. Thus concept, given form by language and verbally communicated, is a process through which creation happens. The throat chakra plays a vital part in enabling us to realize our full potential as human beings.

The sacral chakra is mainly connected to forces which might be described as 'driving' or 'dynamic' (see Chapter 6). In life, eventually, these forces find expression through our throat chakras. The sacral chakra and the throat are, after crown and root, the second most natural and strongly interactive pair within the chakra system.

The major life issues of creativity, sexuality, power and empowerment at the sacral centre demand of us responsibility. They need to find appropriate expression and communication. Responsibility, expression and communication are all attributes connected with the throat chakra. The sacral chakra *needs* the throat in order that fundamental aspects within us can find expression in living. If the throat is, in any way, an afflicted chakra, a great deal of inner frustration may develop, as the power within us will be difficult to channel and focus. If the sacral centre is undeveloped the stream of power flowing to the centre of expression (the throat) will be too weak, intermittent or diffuse. As we saw earlier in this chapter this also hinders the development of the lower will and ego at the solar plexus and the whole being may be too watery and unformed, with 'loop-backs' in the energy system.

Loop-backs

Energy loop-backs in the chakra system happen when development of any chakra is seriously impaired. Loop-backs can be particularly troublesome when they occur because of an imbalance in a major and essential chakra pairing such as that of sacral and throat. Loop-backs between sacral and throat will also affect the solar plexus and heart chakras.

If the sacral is undeveloped the appropriate energy is unavailable to the solar plexus and there is not enough impetus to bring the link energy through to the heart or throat. An important energy pathway may thus remain immature or almost unformed. What power there may be, will fall or loop back into the sacral centre, causing a build-up which has no appropriate channel through which it can find an outlet. The energy which drops back, unchannelled, can form a blockage or energy build-up in the sacral chakra itself, making it overactive. The throat, not receiving the energy it needs from its major partner chakra, will consequently be weak and underactive.

If the energy build-up remains stuck in the sacral centre the being may become very sexually frustrated, power-orientated or violent. If a proportion of the energy seeks release through the solar plexus, without being properly integrated there, the being may manifest as very self-willed or egotistical. If the excess intensity drops back into the root chakra, without being fully grounded, depression, difficulty in relating to life, or excessive materialism and disregard for natural cycles and flow, can manifest.

Physical illnesses and conditions can also be caused by chakra energy loop-backs. In the case of throat and sacral, these might be particularly: ear, throat, thyroid, lymphatic, sexual, menstrual or urinary problems.

Central column breathing (see page 17) helps to keep all pathways open, to minimize and heal chakra blockages, and prevent energy loop-backs. But eventually the essential cause of any vital hiatus needs the recognition and treatment which results from working with chakras as pairs, triads, or individually. (For more specific, individual, chakra work, see my previous book *Working With Your Chakras* in the Bibliography.)

Exercise 27 (page 176) activates the connection between your sacral and throat chakras and helps prevent the most major possible loop-back within the chakra system.

THE SACRAL, SOLAR PLEXUS AND THROAT CHAKRAS

These three chakras are not a triad in the same way as the root, sacral and heart chakras, yet when the sacral works harmoniously with the solar plexus *and* with the throat the healthy result is a natural flow and blending between all three, forming a major chakra system strength.

Case Study: Identity Crisis

Brian had been a star pupil at his comprehensive school. He was able in every educational field and thirsted for knowledge. He was also musical, artistic and good at sport. He seemed to be one of those young people of whom it is said, 'the gods favour him'.

The crowning moment came when Brian won a scholarship to Oxford. His school, his parents, his friends and he himself were pleased and proud. With so many avenues open to him, choosing what to read at university was not easy. Eventually Brian decided on philosophy, politics and ecomomics, feeling that, with such a study behind him, the possibilities for his future career would be wide.

Though Brian's talents, and particularly his prowess on the sports field, had always made him popular and 'one of the gang' (which included young women as well as men), he had never had a serious girlfriend. His parents teased him mildly about this, but accepted that much of his time went into study and games.

The crisis came towards the end of Brian's first university year. His studies had initially gone well, but in his second term Brian realized that he was attracted to, and eventually in love with, a fellow male student. The question of being 'gay' had never occurred to him before and, though his love was reciprocated, he felt himself to be in an emotional tangle and an identity crisis. He knew that, though his parents might eventually understand, they would consider this discovery about him to be the flaw which marked the jewel. He would find their inevitable underlying disappointment very difficult to live with.

Though counselling was available at university, Brian felt so confused that he did not believe it would help him. Endeavouring to cope alone, he ended his relationship and arranged to change his course of study for his second year, so that he would mix in different circles.

In the long vacation, the fact that he needed to work to catch up on knowledge for the new course to which he had transferred gave Brian an excuse to spend long hours alone in his room. His parents felt his stress, but accepted it as relatively normal and inevitable. But the day came when he drank a quantity of wine and took an overdose of aspirin. As it turned out, this was the way in which Brian's psyche chose to call for help, rather than a carefully calculated suicide attempt. Inevitably the whole story came out and, though his parents were supportive and compassionate, Brian slipped into a deep depression and did not return to university.

So far, Brian's life had seemed mapped out – all pathways leading to what the world would term 'success'. Yet the tremendous drive of his sexuality had never been addressed and, because he was intellectually brilliant, he had automatically accepted that he would take up academic study and an academic career.

As part of the treatment for his depression, Brian spent some weeks in a therapeutic community. Here, through group therapy, psychodrama, music, creative writing and art therapy, he was helped to come to terms with his homosexuality. From afternoons spent in creative writing Brian rediscovered his love of literature and a considerable writing talent. When he was well on the way to recovery himself and had also entered into a happy relationship with someone he met at the community, Brian devoted some months of voluntary work to the therapeutic community. Eventually he decided to take a course in media studies, hoping that it would lead to openings for his writing and creative talents.

I met Brian much later in his life, when he was a successful writer but wanted to learn some meditative techniques to aid his creative processes. I have used him as a case study here, because of his identity crisis, the loop-back of energy to his sacral chakra which was responsible for his sexuality going temporarily unconscious and then plunging him suddenly into the midst of its drive for expression, and because instead of having had opportunity to find his own 'note' he had been channelled by traditional expectations and the course of events into a field where, though he was capable, he would never truly express his deeper and sensitive nature.

THE ARCHETYPE: THE WORLD

The archetype chosen for this chapter is 'The World'. We often precede the word 'world' with a possessive personal pronoun. We speak of 'my world', 'your world', 'their world', acknowledging to some extent that, whilst living together in 'the' world, there are many interacting worlds which we all, in different ways, both experience and create.

In spiritual terms the world of earth is the world of physical incarnation. It is the world where we work out much of our destiny and learn the lessons which lead us to a state of wholeness or perfection. Much of our journey is about understanding the relationship of spirit to matter and learning to balance our lives accordingly. The material world can become a spiritual trap. Denial of the material world makes us spiritually ungrounded and perhaps insufficiently aware of the lessons we came into incarnation to learn.

It is important not to confuse the world with the universe. Our world is earth, as it is portrayed on a globe map of 'the world'. The universe is rapidly opening up to us and becoming a part of our world, but it is important to be aware of this interaction and not to assume that our world is the universe. Keeping conceptual boundaries correct, and defining or re-defining our world, actually helps us relate to other worlds and planes.

In traditional Tarot divination the card of 'The World' indicates successful achievement of an aim. Drawing the card in reverse suggests over-attachment to worldly things and an obstacle to be overcome.

EXERCISES

Exercise 26
Linking the Sacral and Solar Plexus Energies

Making sure that you will be undisturbed, sit or stand with your spine straight, your body symmetrically arranged and your legs uncrossed at ankles or knees.

- Begin with central column breathing (see page 17).
- When you feel centred, let the rhythm of your breathing focus your attention into your sacral chakra. Begin to breathe in through the petals of your sacral chakra and out through its stem (five to ten in/out breath sequences).
- Change the focus of your attention to your solar plexus chakra and begin to breathe in through the petals of your solar plexus chakra and out through its stem (five to ten in/out breath sequences).
- Now, once again breathe in through the petals of your sacral chakra, but in the centre of your chakra hold your breath for a count of three before breathing the breath/energy stream up through your central column into the centre of your solar plexus chakra and out through its petals (five to ten in/out breath sequences).
- Breathe in through the petals of your solar plexus chakra. Hold the breath in its centre for a count of three before breathing the breath/energy stream down through your central column into the centre of your sacral chakra and out through its petal (five to ten in/out breath sequences).
- Finish with central column breathing.

Exercise 27
Linking the Sacral and Throat Energies

Making sure that you will be undisturbed, sit or stand with your spine straight, your body symmetrically arranged and your legs uncrossed at ankles or knees.

- Begin with central column breathing (see page 17).
- When you feel centred, use your breath to help you direct the focus of your attention. Begin to breathe in through the petals of your sacral chakra and out through its stem (five to ten in/out breath sequences).

- Change to breathing in through your throat chakra petals and out through its stem (five to ten in/out breaths).
- Return to breathing in through the petals of your sacral chakra, and hold your breath in the centre of the sacral chakra for a count of three. Breathe on up through your central column to the centre of your throat chakra and out through its petals (five to ten in/out breath sequences).
- Breathe in through the petals of your throat chakra, and hold your breath in its centre for a count of three. Breathe down through the central column to the centre of your sacral chakra and out through its petals (five to ten in/out breath sequences)
- Finish with central column breathing.

Exercise 28
Contacting Your Sub-Personalities

The part of us which is already integrated, or which has the vision of what integration can mean, is our inner wise being. The following guided journey suggests that you connect with this being in order to support you in your meeting with your sub-personalities. The inner wise being is such a universal inner symbol that when you ask it to appear it will come, quite naturally, into your visualization. For some people the inner wisdom may take the form of an essence or presence rather than an actual personified being.

Make sure that you will be undisturbed and that you have writing/drawing materials at hand. Provide yourself with a rug or blanket for warmth, then find a relaxed but balanced and supported position for your body.

- Close your eyes . . . Be aware of the rhythm of your breathing and bring that rhythm into your heart centre, thus activating the heart energy on which to travel into your inner landscape . . . Find yourself in a meadow . . .

Activate all your inner senses, so that you see the objects
and colours, hear the sounds, touch the textures, smell
the fragrances and savour the tastes . . .

- Ask for your inner wise being or presence to be with you
  in the meadow . . . Ask that this presence accompany
  you on your journey to the place where your sub-
  personalities dwell . . . Take with you any special object,
  amulet or talisman which helps you to centre and feel
  protected . . . (See entries for 'Amulets' and 'Talismans'
  in the Glossary.)
- Somewhere in your inner landscape, maybe quite close to
  the meadow, there is a river . . . Carrying or wearing your
  talisman and accompanied by your inner wise presence,
  journey now to this river . . .
- As you walk beside the river you will become aware that
  nearby there is a quiet backwater or tributary stream . . .
  Anchored on this backwater or stream is a houseboat – the
  home of your sub-personalities . . .
- As you draw nearer to the boat you may be aware of the
  activity and noise of your sub-personalities . . .
- Stand by and observe your boat . . . What sort of boat is it?
  What is its state of repair and upkeep? What are the
  arrangements for boarding and landing?
- After this initial inspection withdraw a little from the river
  bank and find a comfortable place in which to sit while
  keeping the boat in full view . . . Choose a sun-warmed spot
  and rest your back against a tree or rock . . . Be aware of
  your inner wise presence supporting you . . .
- Ask that not more than three sub-personalities from the
  houseboat prepare to reveal themselves to you . . .
- Insist that the sub-personalities, unless they are an
  inseparable pair, and therefore really represent one
  complete sub-personality, reveal themselves to you one at a
  time . . . When you have met and greeted the first, ask it to
  step to one side as you greet the next . . . The second

personality should then step back to make way for the third . . .

- Observe and greet each sub-personality and let them also observe and greet you . . . Ask each one to tell you their story in brief (how and when they came into being, what they fear, what they require at this time) . . .

- When you have met these three sub-personalities, reflect on whether any two of them need to talk to each other, and ask your wise presence to give you advice. . . Putting the dialogue into effect is something you can do another time. Use this occasion to become aware of what might be of value to your inner growth . . .

- Before asking your sub-personalities to return to their houseboat, consider whether you are willing to make any commitment to further work with them . . . (This might involve: undertaking to return to this place for further dialogue with your sub-personalities; deciding what to do about any requests they have as to their present needs; returning to this place to allow any two sub-personalities to dialogue together; agreeing to give something to a sub-personality, which it requires, in the form of an assurance or symbolic gift and exchanging this for something you may require of it; using your creativity and the support of your inner wise presence to find ways of understanding your sub-personalities and of modifying their weaknesses and harnessing their strengths. Do not commit yourself to anything which you will be unable to follow up on in the near future.)

- Finally, thank your sub-personalities for revealing themselves and ask them to return to the houseboat, giving them any reassurance or promises of further work which you feel able to give at this time . . .

- When the sub-personalities are safely aboard, journey back to the meadow, accompanied by your inner wise presence . . .

- From the meadow return to the rhythm of your breathing

in your heart centre . . . and to your awareness of your
body, your contact with the ground and your normal
surroundings . . . Visualize a cloak of light with a hood
right around you . . . Take your pencils, pens and crayons
and record your journey.

*Note that this journey provides a chance for you to meet not more
than three of your sub-personalities. On subsequent occasions you
can ask to meet three more sub-personalities, but it is wise to limit the
number you meet at any one time. Some sub-personalities manifest
as twins or in some other way as having an inseparable counterpart.
These pairs count as one sub-personality. I have known, for instance,
a Punch and Judy, a bat and ball and a whip and top.*

Exercise 29
Reflecting on the Archetype of The World

For this reflection simply have your writing and drawing
materials at hand and reflect on what the world means to you.

- Consider your ability to balance spiritual and material
  values.
- Reflect further on the questions:
  - 'How do I taste the world? How does the world taste me?'
  - 'How do I see the world? How does the world see me?'
  - 'How do I hear the world? How does the world hear
    me?'

Exercise 30
Sounding Your Note

- Experiment with making different sounds and singing different notes.

- Sing or chant your name, rhythmically.
- Do some drumming.
- Find a Tibetan singing bowl which resonates a healing sound for you (see entry for 'Tibetan Singing Bowls' in the Glossary).
- If you have the opportunity to make sounds out of doors, the experience can be much more powerful or meaningful.

THE COLOURS

The colours for the solar plexus chakra are yellow, gold and rose.

On the positive side, yellow brings clarity and joy to life. A bright clear yellow gives mental and intellectual stimulus.

Negative shades of yellow can be depressing, make for intellectual sluggishness and negatively affect the digestive system.

Gold is the non-metallic colour and positively brings warmth and expansion. It can be very healing to the digestion.

Negative shades of gold absorb energy and have similar effects to negative shades of yellow.

Rose is the colour of rose quartz. Positively, it brings a sense of calm, comfort, security and tenderness. It brings containment for the inner child or for any disturbed sub-personalities and encourages integration.

Negative shades of rose can perpetuate the petulant child and make it difficult to connect with a sense of self-worth.

The colours for the throat chakra are: blue, silver and turquoise. They are all 'cool' colours.

Blue is a colour which calms and heals. It can help to reduce fevers. The usual shade recommended for use at the throat chakra is 'lapis blue'. This brightens, clarifies and contains.

Negative shades of blue can be too cold and without resonance. They can bring a sense of isolation and loneliness.

Silver is the metallic colour. It softens, strengthens and is protective. It brings the feminine principle to a centre which might otherwise be too activated by masculine principle.

Negative shades of silver can be 'cold as steel'. It can also generate sarcasm, cutting, hurtful remarks, and aggression.

Turquoise encourages depth and expansion. It is the colour to use if you want to reach out to wider audiences, work for the media, lecture, or write.

Negatively, shades of turquoise can be oppressive. They can generate loss of compassion and even tyranny.

The colours for the sacral chakra are orange, amber and gold (non-metallic).

Use the colours as suggested in Exercise 8 (page 42) to develop, awaken and heal your chakras.

THE FRAGRANCES

At the solar plexus vetivert and rose quieten, while bergamot and ylang-ylang stimulate. (Bergamot is an ingredient in Earl Grey tea.) Use the quietening fragrances if you have digestive problems such as colitis or ulcers, if you have difficulty when mingling with crowds or travelling on collective transport, and if you are at a transition point in your life. Use the stimulating fragrances if you have a slow metabolism, defective eyesight or fears about change.

At the throat, lavender and hyacinth quieten, whilst patchouli and white musk stimulate. People who have tense, high-pitched, nervous voices usually need the quietening fragrances, as do those who are over-talkative or over-anxious about finding the right work. Those who speak too softly or hardly at all, who are obviously under-achieving in their work and are unfulfilled but confused as to what to do about it, need the stimulating fragrances.

For the sacral chakra the quietening fragrances are rosemary and rose-geranium, and the stimulating ones are musk and amber. See page 43 for suggestions for using the fragrances.

THE CRYSTALS

Refer to page 44 and the Glossary for general guidance on using crystals. The crystals which will best help the issues considered in this chapter are:

Clear Quartz This is a universal crystal, meaning that it can be used at any chakra and to enhance or amplify any purpose or cause. Choose one with clear facets, a good point at one end and a roundedness at the other, to represent the many facets of your identity and the crystal clarity you are aiming towards.

Rose Quartz This crystal, too, can be used for most chakras and chakra work. In its 'massive' form (crystalline, but without clearly defined points or facets), it is comforting and helps to provide a good climate for transformation and integration.

Citrine A bright, clear, yellow citrine will aid the cultivation of clarity, warmth and the sense of self. It is also healing for digestive upsets.

Lapis Lazuli This aids expression of all kinds. It helps the process of co-ordination and integration within the personality, the expression of special talents, and the healing or management of deafness.

PRAYERS OR AFFIRMATIONS

The sacral chakra prayer or affirmation is:

May the unity of humanity with each other and the earth enable true creativity. May release from a sense of sin and unworthiness lead us into the full knowledge of our empowerment as co-creators, at one with, and a part of the Divine.

The solar plexus chakra prayer or affirmation is:

Through the gift of fire, let reason, logic, opinion and assimilation become truly linked to inspiration that we are not bound within limitation and separation.

The throat chakra prayer or affirmation is:

Help us to develop responsibility. May universal truth impregnate causal action so that the voice of humanity may find true harmony with the voice of the earth.

For suggestions on using prayers or affirmations, see page 45.

Chapter 8

Freeing the Spirit:
The Soul, the Spirit, Guides and Angels

Key Issues: Soul and Spirit, Higher and Lower Selves, Guides and
Angels

Chakra Pairs: Solar Plexus and Brow; Solar Plexus and Crown;
Solar Plexus and Heart

Chakra Triad: Solar Plexus, Brow and Crown

Archetypes: Guru and Devotee

This chapter will help you to:
- learn more about the relationship of soul to spirit, and higher
  will to lower will
- gain a greater understanding of communication with guides
  and angels

AREAS OF INFLUENCE

For lists of the areas of influence for the solar plexus chakra
see page 161; page 77 for the heart chakra; and page 20 for
the crown chakra.

The Brow Chakra

Location Above and between the eyes, with a stem at the back of the head

Key Words Spirit, Completeness, Inspiration, Insight, Command

Colours Indigo, Turquoise, Mauve

Element Radium

Body Higher Mental

Glandular Connection Pineal

Quietening Fragrances White Musk, Hyacinth

Stimulating Fragrances Violet, Rose-geranium

Crystals and Gemstones Amethyst, Purple Apatite, Azurite, Calcite, Pearl, Sapphire, Blue and White Fluorite

Prayer or Affirmation

We seek to command ourselves through the inspiration of the command of God. May true insight be enabled and the finite mind be inspired to a knowledge of completion.

SOLAR PLEXUS AND BROW AS A CHAKRA PAIR

The brow chakra is the window through which the flame of our spirit shines, whilst the crown chakra is the gateway to our soul.

By its very nature, spirit is difficult to describe or define. There is also much confusion about the difference between soul and spirit. In some alchemical systems (see Glossary), spirit is seen as yang or masculine whilst soul is considered to be feminine. This is a helpful working definition.

Spirit can thus be considered as pure flame, clear, direct, eternal and initiating. The spirit initiates and commands life and its evolutionary tasks. It seeks completeness, commands action to enable it, and fertilizes inspiration and insight.

Within each one of us there is a spark or essence which never gets clouded. Beyond our behaviour patterns and reactions to life, untouched by flaws of personality, character or morality, even within the most vicious criminal, this spark burns on. When we know this essence in ourselves and honour it in others, we are far less likely to be inhumane.

When the brow chakra is active, it awakens the urge to achieve complete inner harmony of body, mind, emotions, spirit and soul.

Most of us see the things of the spirit as inspirational. Yet the word 'inspiration' also means 'in-breath'. The Greek *pneuma* and the Latin *spiritus* mean both 'spirit' and 'breath'. The brow chakra, then, is also the window through which we breathe inspiration from the Greater Spirit, to fan the flame of our in-dwelling spirit.

Insight links perception with understanding and is the highest level of intuition. The awakened brow centre activates the kind of insight which goes beyond the boundaries of time and space to enable meetings with guides and angels and a wider comprehension of the imponderable mysteries.

The Sanskrit name for the brow chakra is 'Ajna' or 'command'. Through working with the brow chakra we can attain greater spiritual command of our lives.

The element for the brow chakra is radium. This is, perhaps, a difficult element for us to link with spiritual qualities since we know it as a metallic, radioactive element used in X-rays, radiotherapy and the production of luminous materials.

When asked about radium as an element for the brow centre, Gildas replied:

Radium brings power and light. It has a place in breaking down patterns in order to enable re-assembly. It has a high vibrational rate. Its symbolism at the brow centre concerns the facility of functioning on more than one level or dimension, while physically incarnate. It is about the meeting point of light and spirit in matter.

Spirit, by its very nature, is numinous. Unless the brow chakra is firmly linked with other chakras in the chakra team there is a constant danger that the spiritual seeker may develop an over-numinous relationship with life. If we mistakenly see the spiritual journey as one where we concentrate only on developing higher faculties and altered states of consciousness, the personality through which the spirit needs to shine may be too fragmented and fragile a vessel to carry the light. Hence the pairing between solar plexus and brow is an important one indeed.

The solar plexus is connected to vision, but also to identity and personality development (see also Chapter 7). When solar plexus, throat and sacral connections have been made, the powerful radium light of the spirit can truly inspire the personality and activate the aspects of spirit which are bonded in matter.

We have seen (mainly in Chapters 4 and 5) and shall see again, in this chapter and Chapter 9, how the linking of heart to its significant others within the chakra system brings wisdom and love into manifestation. Yet the perspective which spirit adds is one of pure inspiration and illumination.

Working with your solar plexus/brow pairing enhances the potential for your essential, higher and true self to illumine and inspire your integrated personality and for your harmony of being to reach a high level of expression.

SOLAR PLEXUS AND CROWN AS A CHAKRA PAIR

The main link between the brow and crown is that of soul and spirit. The solar plexus forms a pair with the brow *and* with the crown and all three form a triad. Thus the solar plexus connects to both the vision of the spirit and of the soul.

If spirit is yang, then soul is yin. It is receptive to, and integrating of, evolutionary experience. It carries the weight of all experience gathered until all karma has been cleared. During the evolutionary process the integrating thread of the soul also grows in wisdom and vision. This integrating part is the 'higher self' or 'higher will'.

The crown chakra is the window through which we connect with the higher will, and the solar plexus is the seat of the lower will. When higher and lower will are in good relationship and communication with each other, life can become easier and more meaningful.

We tend to see anything 'higher' as an authority and to project on to that authority the qualities of the judgmental, demanding and harsh taskmaster. Higher selves have had a bad press! Part of the success of the partnership between higher and lower will is that the lower will should be sufficiently conscious of itself to seek autonomy. Whilst that process is being worked out, the spiritual path can be bumpy and hazardous. But when we accept the overview, wisdom and compassionate help of the higher self, the light at the end of the spiritual tunnel appears. Our higher selves are not harsh taskmasters heaping karmic burden upon karmic burden. They long for us to be fulfilled, happy and successful in our lives and to work in cooperation with them so that evolution can proceed as smoothly as possible.

Linking the solar plexus and crown means that two important aspects work harmoniously together instead of possibly creating a polarity and pulling against each other.

SOLAR PLEXUS AND HEART AS A CHAKRA PAIR

In the journey of lower will to linking with higher will, the heart brings compassion, wisdom and tenderness to enable the formation of the solar plexus/crown connection, whilst the solar plexus and heart also form a chakra pair.

Full personality integration cannot take place unless the qualities of heart are active. The integrated being has access to heart energy and uses it in the business of life, relationships, feelings and value judgments. The inner being, and particularly the inner child, cannot be empowered until there is heart energy available to direct to the self. True self-worth is both encouraged and tempered by the heart flow, which lifts it from ego-centredness to making 'manifest the glory of God that is within us' (see page 92 for the rest of this quotation from Nelson Mandela's inaugural speech).

SOLAR PLEXUS, BROW AND CROWN AS A CHAKRA TRIAD

The ultimate goal of evolution is the marriage (or re-marriage) of soul with spirit. This can only take place when all karma has been cleared and the full nature and possibilities of life are understood. The solar plexus thus becomes an important bridge-maker, since it digests life, focuses the eye of vision into life, and enables us to attain incarnational consciousness.

Working to activate the solar plexus/brow/crown triad brings a true commitment to the conscious spiritual quest.

WORKING WITH GUIDES AND ANGELS

Connections between the solar plexus and heart, solar plexus and brow and solar plexus and crown, and the activation of the solar plexus/brow/crown triad, strengthen the energetic pathways which make communication with other dimensions safe and possible. It should be noted that communication with guides and angels is a wide topic, more fully discussed in my book, *Working With Guides and Angels* (see Bibliography).

Gildas has described the being and function of guides:

The original spark or soul comes from the Source. In order to become *like* the Source and also to ensure that the Source is not static, the soul takes on incarnation and journeys through many lifetimes in search of evolution. Gradually an overseeing, observing or higher self emerges and then each time an incarnation takes place only a part of the whole becomes personified in order to undergo the further experience which the essence requires in its search for wholeness.

When the soul thread is sufficiently evolved, the wheel of rebirth is no longer its main concern or focus. There is then an opportunity to continue on the path of evolution by being of service in different ways. Guides and communicators have agreed to aid the collective journey by sharing the less finite view and wider perspective seen from other planes of being. This is why we seek individuals on earth with whom to communicate. Our aim is to help in making the experience of incarnation less blinkered or limited in vision for you.

Guides cross the interface between planes in order to communicate. They have different concerns or aims in making their contact with incarnate human beings. For some, the main focus will be healing; for others teaching; whilst yet others will seek to inspire the artist, poet, architect, musician or writer.

Our beings on these planes are more diffuse than are yours on earth. We take on a personality so that we can have more understandable, direct and tender contact with you – but we no longer endure the limitations of personality as you do.

Belief in angels is woven into the fabric of humanity's spiritual search. From untutored reverence through to myths, tribal belief systems and every form of religious practice, angels have been recipients of prayer as well as guests at celebrations and rituals.

Angels bring us light and laughter, as well as enabling our finite minds to arrive at a wider understanding of divinity, infinity and the scheme of the universe.

Many discarnate guides are now suggesting that angels are seeking a more personal relationship with humans. They are eager to teach us about the nature of light and to help us understand the dimension of levity as well as that of gravity.

Guides are part of the human stream of consciousness but angels are not. Guides have been incarnate. Angels will never be incarnate. Guides and humans will never be angels.

The angels manifest Divine Principles or the Archetypes of Higher Qualities for us. When we seek to fulfil the potentials of human living we are dealing with angelic substance.

The word 'angel' means messenger. When interacting with angels you can send messages into the cosmos as well as receive them – the messenger service is two-way.

When asked how we could differentiate between communication which comes from angels and that which comes from guides, Gildas said:

Imagine the notes of bells. The higher, more tinkling notes are those of the angels. The lower notes are those of the guides. Together a whole carillon of bells creates many harmonies.

In order to establish communication with guides and angels we need the throat, brow and crown chakras to be open or active so that we can make our part of the journey to meet these beings of rarer substance. We must journey towards them and not just expect them to come and awaken us. We need an open heart chakra in order to communicate from our inner wisdom to the higher wisdom and so make the best use of guidance. We need an activated solar plexus/brow/crown connection in order to use guidance effectively in our lives.

Exercises 35 and 36 on pages 198–200 are those recommended by Gildas for opening a contact with our guides and angels.

Case Study: Freeing the Spirit

Marion had recently retired. An only child, born when her mother was over forty, Marion had always worked hard in order to support her ageing parents. Her father had died much earlier, her mother about two years before Marion's first visit to me.

Marion had gone on working after her mother died, because she wanted to save money for travel. She had gone from school into banking and had an executive post when she retired. The bank had moved her round a little, but she had never consented, particularly in latter years, to go too far from home. She had longed to see something of the world, but felt a strong duty to her parents and had honoured it without complaint.

Since retirement Marion had travelled to some exotic places. She came to me on the recommendation of a friend because, although her travel had been thrilling and, in some ways, the fulfilment of a dream, she still felt that she was looking for something she had not yet found.

It did not take long to deduce that what Marion really wanted was inner journeying. At first, she just wanted to know more about herself and her psychological make-up. Eventually she began to ask about guides, angels and the spiritual dimension. Never interested in conventional religion, she now began to read widely of philosophy, Buddhism and New Age writings, including channelled guidance and teaching.

Eventually Marion discovered that she could channel beautiful poetry, some of which was published in an anthology. Her story was straightforward in many ways, but opening the windows of her soul and freeing her spirit gave meaning to what might otherwise have seemed a very mundane life. Her ability to meditate and channel beautiful words gave her enormous happiness which shone from her. She confided that many friends had asked if she had acquired a secret lover in her retirement. In some ways, with psychological understanding and spiritual work, she felt she had. She had acquired an inner balance which made her complete, content and radiant in herself.

THE ARCHETYPES: THE GURU AND THE DEVOTEE

The guru and the devotee have been chosen as archetypes for this chapter because, as we seek spiritually, we often need to find a teacher. Gildas has commented that the guru and the devotee belong to the Piscean age. He sees them as self-perpetuating archetypes. The guru remains a guru and the devotee a devotee. The devotee empowers the guru, but the guru does not work towards his/her own redundancy. For the Aquarian age, Gildas encourages us to be eclectic in our search and to favour teachers who seek to empower their pupils and who are content to work towards their own redundancy.

We should not expect our inner guides to be gurus who require slavish obedience either. Our guides wish to give us another perspective, will often offer spiritual teaching and solace, but do not want to live our lives for us or for us to expect them to do so.

There is no formal exercise for contacting the guru or devotee in this chapter. I merely ask you to reflect on these archetypes and the concepts of self-responsibility and inner resources.

EXERCISES

Exercise 31
Linking the Solar Plexus and Brow Energies

Sit or stand with your spine straight, your head well-balanced on your neck, your body symmetrically arranged and with your legs uncrossed at feet or ankles, unless in a cross-legged or lotus position.

- Begin with central column breathing (see page 17)
- Use your breath rhythm to help you focus your attention into your solar plexus chakra. Breathe in through the petals and out through the stem (five to ten in/out breath sequences).
- Focus on your brow chakra. Breathe in through its petals and out through its stem (five to ten in/out breath sequences).
- Focus again on your solar plexus chakra. Breathe in through the petals of your chakra, hold the breath in its centre to a count of three, and breathe on up through your central column to the centre of your brow chakra. Breathe out through your brow chakra petals (five to ten in/out breath sequences).
- Focus on your brow chakra. Breathe in through the petals of your brow chakra. Hold your breath in the centre of your brow chakra to a count of three. Breathe down through your central column into your solar plexus chakra and out through your solar plexus chakra petals (five to ten in/out breath sequences).
- Finish with central column breathing, ending on the down-breath.

Exercise 32
Linking Solar Plexus and Crown Energies

Position yourself as for Exercise 31, above.

- Begin with central column breathing (see page 17).
- Focus on your solar plexus chakra, breathe in through its petals and out through its stem (five to ten in/out breath sequences).
- Still focusing on your solar plexus chakra, breathe in to the centre of your chakra, hold your breath for a count of three, then breathe on up through your central column and out through your crown chakra. (five to ten in/out breath sequences).
- Focus on your crown chakra. Breathe in to the centre of the many-petalled lotus of your crown chakra, and hold your breath to a count of three. Breathe down your central column to the centre of your solar plexus chakra and out through the petals of your solar plexus (five to ten in/out breath sequences).
- Finish with central column breathing, ending on the down-breath.

Exercise 33
Linking the Solar Plexus and Heart Energies

Position yourself as for Exercise 31 (see page 195).

- Begin with central column breathing (see page 17).
- Focus on your solar plexus chakra. Breathe in through its petals and out through its stem (five to ten in/out breath sequences).
- Breathe in through the petals of your solar plexus chakra, hold the breath in its centre for a count of three, then

breathe up through your central column to the centre of your heart chakra and out through the petals of your heart chakra (five to ten in/out breath sequences).

- Breathe in through the petals of your heart chakra and out through its stem (five to ten in/out breath sequences).
- Breathe in through the petals of your heart chakra to its centre. Hold your breath for a count of three, breathe down through your central column into the centre of your solar plexus chakra and out through its petals (five to ten in/out breath sequences).
- Finish with central column breathing, ending on the down-breath.

Exercise 34
Connecting the Solar Plexus, Brow and Crown Triad

Position yourself as for Exercise 31 (see page 195).

- Begin with central column breathing (see page 17).
- Breathe in through the petals of your solar plexus chakra and out through its stem (five to ten in/out breath sequences).
- Breathe in through the petals of your brow chakra and out through its stem (five to ten in/out breath sequences).
- Breathe in deeply through the petals of your solar plexus chakra to its centre, hold your breath for a count of three, and breathe up through your central column into the centre of your brow chakra and out through its petals. Now breathe in through the petals of your brow chakra to its centre, sustaining the in-breath as you visualize the breath energy going up through your central column, through your crown chakra, down the front of your body. And breathe out as you visualize the energy going into the centre of your solar plexus chakra and then finally out through its stem (five x two in/out breath sequences).

- Finish with central column breathing, ending on the down-breath.

Exercise 35
Establishing an Inner Meeting Place for Work with Guides and Angels

Making sure that you will be undisturbed, with a blanket for warmth, and writing and drawing materials at hand, sit or lie in a comfortable, but symmetrically balanced position.

- Be aware of the rhythm of your breathing . . . Gradually bring the breath into your heart centre and travel into your inner landscape, finding yourself in a meadow . . . Activate all your inner senses so that you see the objects and colours . . . smell the fragrances . . . hear the sounds . . . touch the textures . . . savour the tastes . . .
- From your meadow look out at the surrounding landscape . . . Nearby there is a winding pathway which leads into hills and continues up into some mountains . . .
- You are going to take this pathway, knowing that you are going to a plateau which is near the top of one of the mountains but not beyond the tree line . . .
- Make your way to the plateau in your own time, noting the scenery through which you pass as you go . . .
- At the plateau take time to explore . . . You will probably find a source of clear running water from which to refresh yourself and there may be a small sanctuary or traveller's rest . . . There may be a place of natural sanctuary with a sun-warmed rock against which to rest your back and look out over the landscape . . . As you explore the plateau you are looking for a place where you are happy to sit and wait, with an open heart and an open expectation . . .
- When you have settled yourself in the place of your choice,

enjoy the peace ... If there is a question in your heart, hold it there, pondering it in a relaxed way ...

- At this stage do not expect or invite a presence to be with you, but rather seek to establish this meeting place ... You have made your part of the journey ... This territory is yours but be aware that it is also part of the bridge to other worlds and planes ...
- Stay here for not more than ten minutes ... When you are ready to return, drink again from the water source ... Make your way back to the meadow ...
- From the meadow return to the awareness of your breath in your heart centre ... to the awareness of your body and your contact with the ground ... to your outer surroundings ... Visualize a cloak of light with a hood right around you ...
- Take time to record your journey in words or drawing.

Exercise 36
Drawing Your Guardian Angel Closer to you

Making sure that you will be undisturbed, sit or lie in a comfortable but symmetrically balanced position. Have ready a blanket for warmth, and writing and drawing materials for recording your journey.

- Be aware of the rhythm of your breathing ... Gradually bring that rhythm into your heart chakra ... Travel on your heart energy into your inner landscape ... Find yourself in a meadow ... Awaken your inner senses, so that you see the objects and colours around you ... hear the sounds ... touch the textures ... smell the fragrances ... and savour the tastes ...
- In your meadow there is a rainbow ... You can actually experience the place where the rainbow begins or ends ... All the brilliant, translucent colours of the spectrum are

pouring down to and into the earth . . . Stand in this
rainbow light and, as you experience the colours, ask that
the particular colour which will help to draw your
guardian angel closer to you may flood into you and bring
you healing and harmony . . .

- Leave the rainbow, but, as you walk out into the meadow
once more, the colour of your choice, (or the colour
which has chosen you) will continue to surround you . . .
Feel yourself beginning to soften a little at the edges and
merge into the colour . . .

- Let the colour become soft in texture around you, like the
gentle brushing and protection of an angel's wings . . .
Feel lightened and protected, but also free as the colour
becomes your guardian angel, gently holding you . . .

- Your angel may have more than one colour in its light . . .
Let these develop and feel their protective quality . . .

- Remember a time in your life when you felt that, although
you were in some kind of danger, or at risk, there was a
protective influence around you . . . Thank your guardian
angel for that intervention . . . Ask your guardian angel to
make you more and more conscious of the protection and
help which it holds out for you at all times . . .

- When you are ready to return from this experience make
your journey through your meadow with the sense of your
angel behind you or at your side . . . Return to an awareness
of the rhythm of your breathing in your heart centre . . .
Become aware of your physical body and of your contact
with the ground . . . Bring the sense of your guardian
angel's presence right through into your outer world . . .
Remember those colours and the strong, but gentle
presence of your guardian angel whenever you feel anxious
or in need.

THE COLOURS

The colours for the brow chakra are indigo, turquoise and mauve.

Indigo is a colour we find difficult to perceive and describe; it is neither purple, nor navy blue. It is intense and deep, sometimes almost black, but always containing a touch of red. For chakra work it is translucent, as the colour would appear when sunlight passes through stained glass. Learning to differentiate indigo is, in itself, a good exercise for opening and awakening the brow chakra.

Positively, indigo brings peace, confidence and a sense of security.

Negatively, it can be heavy, or become associated with the 'dark night of the soul'.

Mauve at the brow centre, is dark in tone – a hue between lavender and purple.

Positively, it helps to connect the numinous with the tangible and raises the spirits.

Negatively, it can be cold and absorb energies, so creating a sense of lethargy.

Turquoise is bright – the colour of the gemstone of the same name.

Positively, turquoise feeds us spiritually and also acts as spiritual protection.

Negatively, it can cloud our judgment and make us feel distanced from life.

The colours for the solar plexus chakra are yellow, gold and rose.

The colours for the crown chakra are violet, white and gold.

The colours for the heart chakra are spring green, rose and rose amethyst.

Use the colours as suggested in Exercise 8 (page 42) to develop, awaken and heal your chakras.

THE FRAGRANCES

White musk and hyacinth quieten the brow chakra, while violet and rose-geranium stimulate it. If you have anxiety about your spiritual progress or over-zealously use meditational and spiritual practices you may over-stimulate your brow chakra, signalled by headaches in and around the chakra area. In such cases the quietening fragrances should be used to help the flow and movement within the brow to become calmer and steadier.

If you are new to spiritual development, gently use the stimulating fragrances to encourage your brow chakra to open and function well for you. For the solar plexus chakra the quietening fragrances are vetivert and rose, and the stimulating ones are bergamot and ylang-ylang. For the heart chakra the quietening fragrances are sandalwood and rose, and the stimulating ones are pine and honeysuckle. For the crown chakra the quietening fragrances are rosemary and bergamot and the stimulating ones are violet and amber.

Blending the fragrances, as suggested on page 43, will help to connect the chakra pairs and the chakra triad.

THE CRYSTALS

Refer to page 44 and the Glossary for general guidance on using crystals. The crystals which will best help the issues considered in this chapter are:

Amethyst to enhance spiritual awareness and encourage vision. It is also a protective stone, which absorbs and transforms negativity.

Sapphire to strengthen spiritual awareness and communication. It facilitates communication with guides and angels.

White Flourite to help make connections between the brow and solar plexus chakras. It helps to prevent depression and disillusionment.

Ellestial crystals To help awaken the spirit and matter and to ensure links with the highest available guidance. These cystals encourage angelic presences to be around you and in your life.

PRAYERS OR AFFIRMATIONS

The brow chakra prayer or affirmation is:

We seek to command ourselves through the inspiration of the command of God. May true insight be enabled and the finite mind be inspired to a knowledge of completion.

The crown chakra prayer or affirmation is:

Through surrender and release, let the incoming will be truly the will of God working within us and through us and leading us increasingly to knowledge of mystical union and mystical marriage.

The solar plexus chakra prayer or affirmation is:

Through the gift of fire, let reason, logic, opinion and assimilation become truly linked to inspiration that we are not bound within limitation and separation.

The heart chakra prayer or affirmation is:

In the golden centre of the rose of the heart may tender compassion be linked to unconditional love. May true detachment enable growth and continuity. Through the understanding of birth within death and death within birth may there be transformation.

For suggestions on using prayers or affirmations, see page 45.

Chapter 9

Inner Wisdom:
Getting Older and Wiser

Key Issues: Inner Wisdom, Ageing and Sageing, Fullness of Being
Chakra Pairs: Heart and Crown, Heart and Throat
Archetypes: The Sage and the Crone

This chapter will help you to:
- come to terms with the ageing process
- learn more about heart-centred wisdom
- aid the activation and expression of the wisdom carried by your soul stem from other lifetimes

AREAS OF INFLUENCE

For lists of the areas of influence for the heart chakra see page 77; page 161 for the throat chakra; and page 20 for the crown chakra.

HEART AND CROWN AS A CHAKRA PAIR

When we consider chakras in isolation they stand strongly for the activation of certain qualities. When they are linked to another chakra with which they form a natural pair, one chakra aspect may be emphasized, or another and deeper aspect of a chakra may emerge.

We have seen that the heart chakra is connected to feeling and feeling has been defined as a second level of emotion (see page 127–30). When heart and crown are energetically linked, the quality which emerges is that of wisdom. The wisdom of the soul calls out to and awakens the inner wisdom, and vice versa.

Gildas has said that, paradoxically, we are most likely to form a successful link with our higher guides when our inner wisdom has been activated. As we saw when discussing the archetypes of guru and devotee (page 194) the true guide does not want us to be dependent upon him/her. Like good and more experienced friends, they want to offer us the benefit of their wider perspective, without imposition, over-parenting, invasion or judgment. When we can receive their teachings, question and interpret them, use them for information, but also make our own responsible, informed decisions, guidance works well. When we *need* a guide too desperately, because we cannot cope with life, then we may go to a channel for guidance but our own higher guide will not come through until some of our crises of choice are over.

Linking heart to crown encourages us to use our support systems judiciously and helps our inner wisdom to flourish. It awakens the heart of our being in which lies that integrity which lights our path and is the core of our strength.

As this link strengthens, we often find that we have access to wisdom or even skills which we have not consciously learned. This might be said to be the positive side of karma. In other lifetimes we have learned much. Sometimes an aspect of the doctrine of many lifetimes which people find puzzling is that it seems that each time we incarnate we forget what we have learned previously and need to start again. This is because each life has new lessons but one of the great advantages of working with our chakras is that we gradually activate, or re-activate, our highest potential.

The heart/crown link is the catalyst to the sensing of our wider being. We may not remember specific past lives, but we will realize that we have access to a fount of knowledge far greater than anything we have learned by rote, patience or persistence in this present lifetime.

HEART AND THROAT AS A CHAKRA PAIR

If the heart/crown link activates wisdom, then the heart/throat connection activates our ability to know that we have it and to express it in our lives and for others around us, without being dogmatic, self-aggrandizing or patronizing, but with compassion and discernment.

Our society has lost respect for the sagacity of age. Currently the growing proportion of ageing people is considered to be a social problem and a financial burden. The elderly can feel that they deplete resources and that their life-experience means little. When this is believed strongly enough, it can become a self-fulfilling prophecy. The elderly become child-like, regressed and dependent in an undignified way.

If we respected the rich resources, particularly of a spiritual kind, which the elderly can possess, then the actual economic problems of an ageing population might be more easily resolved.

In Native American Indian tradition, the spiritual continuity and growth of the tribe depends upon the wisdom, teaching and initiation which the grandmothers and grandfathers have to give. Age is a mantle of dignity and respect. New traditions grow naturally and creatively from the old, without the disadvantage and potential wastage of youth-based innovation.

At a spiritual and soul level, and within the concept of many lifetimes, ageing and sageing have another dimension. We each have the crone or sage within us. If we can get beyond the current tendency to find the ageing process embarrassing, frightening, degrading or disgusting, then we will be better able to relate to the old soul within us and to draw on the wisdom stored in the collective unconscious of the whole of humanity (see also Chapter 11). We might even get beyond the point at which, as a family of beings, we have to repeat the same mistakes over and over again. When we contact the old soul within, our management of the personal ageing process is bound to improve.

Case Study: Living Wisely

Joan was in her late sixties when I first met her. She was distressed because she felt that her family and her grand-children saw her as 'silly and unintelligent'.

Uneducated herself, Joan had nursed a sick husband and an ageing mother. Alongside this, she had worked hard to make sure that there were financial resources available for the sound education of her son and her two daughters. They had done well, had all gone to college or university and now had flourishing careers, good marriages, lovely homes and healthy children. They lived modern lives at a hectic pace, surrounded by computers, mobile phones and fast cars.

Joan had lost touch with her sense of accomplishment in nurturing her family's talents and in providing so well for them. She felt redundant, that she had no proper communication with the young people and that they belittled her. It later turned out that the latter was not objectively true, but it was true for her, in the moment, and thererefore had to be dealt with. In fact, Joan had also been successful in imparting a deep warmth to her children and they were as anxious about her as she was about herself.

Joan bravely came to some workshops and became interested in healing, for which she had a considerable gift. Gradually she began to offer healing and solace, and the natural counsel of an experienced lifer, to friends in the village where she lived, building quite a reputation for herself. To her amazement and delight, many young people began to gather at her home, seeking not only healing for themselves or their children, but advice on all matters from the mundane to the spiritual. They liked to be with her, found her unshockable and often repaid her in kind, by including her in family events and activities or helping, as she got older, with shopping and gardening.

Inevitably her own family noticed changes in Joan. When they came to visit there was often a houseful of people. They saw the respect in which their mother and grandmother was held and they, too, began to ask her for healing and advice.

In awakening her healing talents Joan had worked with her chakras and all the energetic connections, particularly those between heart and crown and heart and throat. As her healing flowed, so did her natural wisdom which struck a chord with the young around her, causing them instinctively to value and reinstate the crone in their village and their lives.

Joan is now older than she cares to admit, but still active, still dignified and still sought-out and respected.

THE ARCHETYPES: THE CRONE AND THE SAGE

As we have seen, our society neglects the archetypes of the crone and the sage. We pursue too arduously the fountain or elixir of eternal youth. This is partly a sign of our being out-of-touch with natural rhythms and cycles – and partly our fear of mortality and extinction.

So many aspects of life become easier to understand or to

live through when we believe in an eternity of being. The concept of many lifetimes can make us aware that no experience is ever wasted and that we are not under pressure to complete everything we want to do in one lifetime. Such beliefs make it not only easier to live, but easier to die – for we can know that our essence lives on.

The archetypes of the sage and the crone personify continuity of experience and the wisdom which endures.

EXERCISES

Exercise 37
Linking Heart and Crown Energies

Making sure that you will be undisturbed, sit or stand with your spine straight, your body symmetrical and your legs uncrossed at knees or ankles, unless using a cross-legged or lotus position.

- Begin with central column breathing (see page 17).
- Focus on your heart chakra and breathe in through its petals and out through its stem (five to ten in/out breath sequences).
- Breathe in through the petals of your heart chakra, hold your breath for a count of three in its centre, and then breathe upward through your central column to your crown chakra and out through your crown (five to ten in/out breath sequences).
- Breathe in through the petals of your crown chakra, hold your breath in the centre of your crown chakra for a count of three, and then breathe down into the centre of your heart chakra and out through its petals (five to ten in/out breath sequences).

- Finish with central column breathing, ending on the down-breath.

Exercise 38
Linking Heart and Throat Energies

Position yourself as for Exercise 37, above.

- Begin with central column breathing (see page 17).
- Focus on your heart chakra and breathe in through its petals and out through its stem (five to ten in/out breath sequences).
- Breathe in through the petals of your heart chakra, to its centre. Hold your breath for a count of three, and then breathe up through your central column into the centre of your throat chakra and out through its petals (five to ten in/out breath sequences).
- Breathe in through the petals of your throat chakra and out through its stem (five to ten in/out breath sequences).
- Breathe in through the petals of your throat chakra to its centre, and hold your breath for a count of three. Breathe down through your central column into the centre of your heart chakra and out through its petals (five to ten in/out breaths).
- Finish with central column breathing, ending on the down-breath.

Exercise 39
Creating a Place of Inner Wisdom

Making sure that you will be undisturbed, create a quiet space for yourself and lie or sit comfortably in a position in which your body is symmetrically arranged.

- Practise central column breathing (see page 17). When you feel centred and peaceful, breathe in at the petals of your crown chakra and out through the petals of your heart . . .
- Visualize your heart chakra opening up like a rose in perfect bloom . . . Imagine travelling to the golden centre of this rose . . . In the golden centre of the rose there is a still point of wisdom and knowing . . . Find this still point and remain in touch with it for five to ten minutes . . . (If your attention wanders, just quietly keep returning to the golden centre of the rose . . .) Know that when you return you will be able to see any problems in your life from a new perspective . . .
- When you are ready, return to an awareness of your breath coming in at the crown of your head and out through the petals of your heart chakra . . . Let the petals of your heart centre gradually close in . . . Feel the contact of your feet with the ground beneath . . . Take your sense of inner peace with you as you resume your normal life once more . . .

Exercise 40
Considering the Inner Crone or Sage

- For this consideration, simply go within, without a formal guided journey . . .
- Imagine meeting with an ancient female or masculine wise figure . . .
  - What gift do you want to give this figure?
  - What gift do you wish to receive from it?
  - What question do you want to ask?
  - What does your inner ancient figure require from you?

THE COLOURS

The colours for the heart chakra are spring green, rose and rose amethyst.

The colours for the throat chakra are blue, silver and turquoise.

The colours for the crown chakra are: violet, white and gold.

Use the colours as suggested in Exercise 8 (page 42) to develop, awaken and heal your chakras.

THE FRAGRANCES

For the heart chakra the quietening fragrances are sandalwood and rose, and the stimulating ones are pine and honeysuckle. For the throat chakra the quietening fragrances are lavender and hyacinth and the stimulating ones are patchouli and white musk. For the crown chakra the quietening fragrances are rosemary and bergamot, and the stimulating ones are violet and amber.

Blending the fragrances, as suggested on page 43, will help to connect the chakra pairs.

THE CRYSTALS

Refer to page 44 and the Glossary for general guidance on using crystals. The crystals which will best help the issues considered in this chapter are:

Snowflake Obsidian Linked to the cycles of birth, death and rebirth, this stone brings stamina and wisdom.

Peacock Stone Sometimes called Bornite or Chalcopyrites, this stone aids the recall of skills which have been known and practised in another lifetime, or which are stored in the collective unconscious. This particularly applies to the revival of ancient healing skills.

PRAYERS OR AFFIRMATIONS

The heart chakra prayer or affirmation is:

In the golden centre of the rose of the heart may tender compassion be linked to unconditional love. May true detachment enable growth and continuity. Through the understanding of birth within death and death within birth may there be transformation.

The throat chakra prayer or affirmation is:

Help us to develop responsibility. May universal truth impregnate causal action so that the voice of humanity may find true harmony with the voice of the earth.

The crown chakra prayer or affirmation is:

Through surrender and release, let the incoming will be truly the will of God working within us and through us and leading us increasingly to knowledge of mystical union and mystical marriage.

For suggestions on using prayers or affirmations, see page 45.

Chapter 10

As Above, So Below:
Spirituality and Divinity

Key Issue: Spiritual Manifestation
Chakra Triad: Throat, Brow and Crown
Archetype: The Divine

This chapter will help you to:
- learn more about the process of spiritual manifestation
- gain a greater understanding of the process of position synchronicity
- reflect on Divinity

AREAS OF INFLUENCE

For lists of the areas of influence for the throat chakra see page 161; page 186 for the brow chakra; and page 20 for the crown chakra.

THROAT, BROW AND CROWN AS A CHAKRA TRIAD

The throat chakra is a gateway chakra: the sevenfold chakra system is sub-divided into two interacting groups and the throat is a member of both. As one of the five lower chakras, it is related to an element, a developmental age and a sense. As the first of the three upper chakras, it is concerned with transpersonal expression and has connections to the higher self, spirit and soul.

When the three upper chakras are open, and in communication as a triad, we often experience an increasing sense of the need to serve humanity, without living in isolation. Service to the collective becomes a necessary and intrinsic part of self-growth and awareness.

The transpersonal psychologist Maslow spoke about self-actualization. He felt that, when growth processes and necessary healing reached a certain point, every part of our being could find expression. The blueprint with which we come into incarnation would be actualized. Probably a totally self-actualized person has little need to remain longer in incarnation – and, being self-actualized, would finish the task in hand and die gracefully. However, there can be times in our lives when we feel that we are 'firing on all cylinders'. This can be cyclical, or part of the spiral of growth. Once attained it may fade again or become elusive for a while, but when we have touched it, even briefly, we know that we are capable of manifesting our full spiritual selves whilst in incarnation.

Energetically speaking, self-actualization happens when there is harmony within the whole chakra team – but it is particularly encouraged when the throat/brow/crown triad is active.

The archetype or essence of the Divine is abstract. When we personify or define it too closely we both limit it and endow it with false powers. That which is infinite cannot be defined. A religion which is built on the image of an old bearded man, sitting on a throne, writing down judgments in a huge book, has not 'come of age'. It is limited, patriarchal and immature. The throat chakra, in its triad with brow and crown, urges us to come of age, spiritually.

Religions which need many figures, both masculine and feminine, in order to express the range within the Divine, have often been rather derogatorily labelled Pantheistic – but that which is infinite must also have infinite facets which subscribe to the whole. Learning the thousand names of the Divine seems to encompass more possibilities than the vision of the old man on the throne.

SPIRITUAL MANIFESTATION

Our apparent need to control and define is an obstacle to spiritual manifestation. That which is abstract, diffuse and defies definition can only truly inspire us and aid our becoming when we let it be as it is, or consciously use open-ended definitions.

One function, then, of the crown chakra is to hold the diffuse and unnamed potential. When the crown, brow and throat are linked, there can be a constant flow of the unnamed potential from the ketheric plane at the crown, through to the higher mental plane at the brow chakra, and then on to the mental or manifestational plane at the throat chakra.

The higher mental plane is also abstract in its nature, but it is the plane on which energies from the ketheric begin to be apprehended by us and to take form. The Divine Principles move us inwardly, before we name them and use them as a life model. The angelic beings, carrying the Divine Principles into pre-manifestational form for us, touch us lightly. As these energies come through to the mental plane, they are named. Once named, they come into existence on our material plane and we work with them as archetypes.

What does this mean for us in our lives? Dealing with abstractions is not easy. I can only suggest that:

- We should not seek to over-define ourselves.
- We should never declare anything to be impossible. There seems to be much truth in the saying: 'Everything is possible under the sun.'
- We should value more and more, the art and practice of play. When we sustain an ability to play, creativity flows and we constantly explore the worlds of wonder and magic. Delight in new combinations enables discovery, from ideas through to colours, shapes and the highly manifestational world of design, furnishing, gadgetry and the way we dress.
- We should look to the world of music. Musicians and composers never run out of new combinations of notes and sounds which produce more and more harmonies to delight our ears.
- In order to let go of the insecurities which fuel our tendency to control and over-decline, we should trust that the blueprint of the Infinite is powered by love.

Case Study: Spiritual Manifestation

Joshua was mentally challenged. Not all the horrific details of his early childhood were known, but he had been physically abused and severely neglected. He was taken into care and then fostered and finally adopted by a warm and loving couple who had been unable to have children of their own.

With love, care and security, Joshua moved from being a very frightened, imprisoned child to a more confident young person reaching out to his full, if comparatively limited, potential. When he was fifteen years old, his mother consulted Gildas about Joshua's obsessive habit of ordering everything. All his possessions had to be laid out in certain patterned and ordered ways. He could fly into rages if anything was moved. Whilst this pattern related mostly to

Joshua's own room and possessions, Nesta and Mike, his adoptive parents, had honoured it, but now Joshua had begun to take more part in everyday household tasks and his need for order was impinging on them all. The cutlery drawer had become a focus for rages and tantrums and sometimes for hours spent obsessively arranging the objects in it.

Gildas felt that, besides Joshua's obvious psychological wounds and misaligned emotional body, he had lost the instinctual link to his higher-self blueprint. This link can be helped and healed when the throat/brow/crown triad is activated. In his ordering activities Joshua was not only seeking security and control in his life, but was over-defining himself. As he had entered the developmental age range for the throat chakra his need for control had been exacerbated.

Obviously we could not teach Joshua complex theories about the chakras. But he loved crystals, colours, fragrances, sounds and music. Nesta got an amethyst and an iron pyrites sun for Joshua and encouraged him to wear clothes in the blue, mauve and purple range. She mixed him his own special bath and massage oil of jojoba carrying oil, to which four drops each of lavender, white musk, rose-geranium, violet and bergamot essential oil concentrates had been added. She also gave him, at Gildas' suggestion, a tape of pan pipe music, since the clearly definable sounds of the pipes have combinations in them which resonate to the throat/brow/crown triad.

Over a period of time these treatments, plus a great deal of love and patience from Nesta and Mike, brought about a change in Joshua. Nesta particularly noticed that if she played the pipe music when Joshua started his ordering rituals, his attention could be more easily diverted or channelled into other activities. Eventually he became comfortable with far less order in his possessions and even developed a sense of humour about his need.

I have used Joshua as an illustration here, because it is easy to feel that the throat/brow/crown connection is spiritually sophisticated. Instead, it can even be developed at a relatively unconscious level, through exposure to sound, colour and crystals.

EXERCISES

Exercise 41
Connecting the Throat/Brow/Crown Triad

Sit or stand with your spine straight, your body symmetrically arranged and your legs uncrossed at knees or ankles unless using a cross-legged or lotus posture.

- Begin with central column breathing (see page 17).
- Breathe in through the petals of your throat chakra and out through its stem (five to ten in/out breath sequences).
- Breathe in through the petals of your throat chakra, hold the breath in the centre of your throat chakra for a count of three, sustain the in-breath as you move up through the central column to the centre of your brow chakra and breathe out through the petals of your brow chakra (five to ten in/out breath sequences).
- Breathe in through the petals of your brow chakra, hold the breath in the centre of your brow chakra for a count of three, then sustain the in-breath as you move the energy up through your central column, into your crown chakra and out through the top of your head (five to ten in/out breath sequences).
- Take a deep in-breath through the crown of your head, into your central column, and, sustaining the in-breath, visualize the energy going out through the petals of your brow chakra, and in through the petals of your throat

chakra. Then finally breathe the energy out through the stem of your throat chakra (five to ten in/out breath sequences).

- Finish with central column breathing, ending on the down-breath.

Sounding

Exercise 30 (page 180) gives suggestions for sounding your own note. For this chakra triad, follow those same suggestions but, as you listen to your own sounding, be aware of notes which resonate to your throat, brow and crown chakra, the full chord for the chakra triad will be harmonious.

THE COLOURS

The colours for the throat chakra are blue, silver and turquoise.

The colours for the brow chakra are indigo, turquoise and mauve.

The colours for the crown chakra are violet, white and gold.

Use the colours as suggested in Exercise 8 (page 42) to develop, awaken and heal your chakras.

THE FRAGRANCES

For the throat chakra the quietening fragrances are lavender and hyacinth, and the stimulating ones are patchouli and white musk. For the brow chakra the quietening fragrances are white musk and hyacinth, and the stimulating ones are violet and rose-geranium. For the crown chakra the quietening fragrances are rosemary and bergamot, and the stimulating ones are violet and amber.

Blend the fragrances, as suggested on page 43. (See also the case study on page 217.)

THE CRYSTALS

Refer to page 44 and the Glossary for general guidance on using crystals. The crystals which will best help the issues considered in this chapter are:

Amethyst To absorb and transform negativity and aid the making of links between chakras.

Iron Pyrites Sun To remind us of our instinctual links to our higher selves and our spiritual blueprint.

Diamond Symbolizing perfection and clarity, diamonds draw us towards our highest potential and encourage the higher will to illumine the personality.

PRAYERS OR AFFIRMATIONS

The throat chakra prayer or affirmation is:

Help us to develop responsibility. May universal truth impregnate causal action so that the voice of humanity may find true harmony with the voice of the earth.

The brow chakra prayer or affirmation is:

We seek to command ourselves through the inspiration of the command of God. May true insight be enabled and the finite mind be inspired to a knowledge of completion.

The crown chakra prayer or affirmation is:

Through surrender and release, let the incoming will be truly the will of God working within us and through us and leading us increasingly to knowledge of mystical union and mystical marriage.

For suggestions on using prayers or affirmations see page 45.

Chapter 11

All My Relations:
In Harmony with Nature

Key Issues: Inter-Species Relationships; Fairies and Nature Spirits; Morphic Resonance

Chakra Pairs: Throat and Alter Major; Alter Major and Crown; Alter Major and Root

Archetypes: Pan and Flora

This chapter will help you to:
- learn more about our interaction with other species, fairies and nature spirits
- gain a greater understanding of self-healing processes
- have hope for the growth of consciousness in humanity and understand the part each individual may play in this

---

AREAS OF INFLUENCE

For lists of the areas of influence for the crown chakra see page 20; page 161 for the throat chakra; and page 19 for the root chakra.

The Alter Major Chakra

Location Petals in the area of the nose. Positive energy centre in its stem, which is where the back of the head begins to bend round, corresponding with the 'old' or 'lizard' brain, before the division into right and left hemispheres

Key Words Instinct, Resonance, Duality, Devic Nature, Healing

Colours Brown, Yellow Ochre, Olive Green

Element Wet Earth

Sense Smell

Body Instinctual and Lower Causal

Glandular Connection Adrenals

Quietening Fragrances Musk, Cedarwood

Stimulating Fragrances Violet, Rose-Geranium

Crystals and Gemstones Carnelian, Tiger's Eye, Snowflake Obsidian, Fossils, Peacock Stone (sometimes called Bornite or Chalcopyrites)

Prayer or Affirmation

Through engagement with our Devic Nature may we move from duality and split, to oneness and unity.

THE ALTER MAJOR CHAKRA

Since the alter major chakra is a lesser-known chakra, let us consider it alone, before moving on to its chakra pairings.

An 'alta major' chakra is described in the writings of Alice Bailey (see Bibliography). 'Alta' means 'higher', whereas 'alter' means 'other'. Some Eastern yogic systems also include a chakra at the back of the head which is not related to a specific number of petals or to a Sanskrit vowel sound (as are the seven classical chakras).

With the other seven chakras there is a sequential progression from lower to higher, according to their vibrational rate and their relationship to the upright human body. The placement of the alter major is thus out of sequence. Although situated between the throat and the brow, its vibrational rate comes between those of the root and sacral chakras. Its element is a combination of earth and water; it shares the sense of smell with the root chakra and its glandular connection with the solar plexus.

Whereas the other chakras have a positive electric or magnetic polarity in their petals and a negative polarity in their stems, the alter major chakra is the only one to have a reversed polarity. The energy flow moves from the back of the head to the front (see diagram, page 7).

Working with the alter major chakra can be instrumental in awakening instinctual alertness. Energetically, the alter major is linked to the old brain cortex, or 'lizard brain'. This means that it can put us in touch with the non-verbal message system which protects us from, or warns us of, danger. This is similar to the instinct which causes rats to leave a ship or pit ponies to refuse to enter a coal-seam, well in advance of any other warnings that something is wrong. As humans, if we 'happen' to get up and leave the room just before the ceiling falls in over the chair where we were sitting we explain it away as 'lucky chance'. We say, 'my number wasn't up yet', or 'my guardian angel was working hard'. It is difficult for us to believe that these happenings come from a non-verbal signalling which can be more consciously cultivated. If this sense had not been so universally lost or dishonoured, our planet might not now be facing the threat of imminent disaster. Warnings tend only to be accepted if they have been scientifically or intellectually proven. Prophets working intuitively or instinctually are not respected and may become figures of fun.

The alter major chakra is the window through which we can connect to the phenomenon which Rupert Sheldrake (see Bibliography) named as 'morphic resonance' and linked to the 'hundredth monkey' theory. If one monkey on an island learns to wash potatoes and then teaches another, who teaches another, as soon as one hundred monkeys on the island wash potatoes, all the monkeys everywhere will start to wash potatoes without having gone through a learning or modelling process. (The figure 'one hundred' represents an optimum number or proportion.)

Jung wrote extensively about the 'collective unconscious' (see Bibliography). He theorized that everything which humans do, or have ever done, affects and impinges on each one of us.

These energies suggest exciting possibilities for the role of the individual in collective change. With sophisticated communication systems, the 'optimum number' may be more easily reached. In recent years world days of prayer, peace, meditation and humour have played a considerable role in changing our awareness and encouraging us to share resources. What is not so universally known is that working with the alter major chakra and its chakric pairs increases the efficiency of morphic resonance and the 'creative minority'. When enough people recognize this, and work with these connections, then quantum leaps will surely happen in our time.

ALTER MAJOR AND THROAT AS A CHAKRA PAIR

Connecting the alter major and throat chakras as a pair leads to an increase in our abilities to heal ourselves; to have access to past, stored knowledge (including the record of our own evolution); and to communicate with other species, including nature spirits, fairies and devic beings.

The throat chakra is a dual chakra (see page 161) and the alter major is linked to the archetype of Pan who has much to teach us about duality. Problems brought about by dualities and oppositions in life often underlie the process of dis-ease. Within each one of us there is a natural self-healing mechanism. When we are really ill this self-healing mechanism becomes depressed. Much healing, whether allopathic or complementary, aims to some degree to 'kick-start' or 'jump-lead' the self-healing mechanism.

Research shows that we can consciously influence the so-called autonomous systems of the body when we learn to activate the right side of the brain. When we engage deliberately with our self-healing mechanisms, the elementals within us are enabled to help our bodies back to health and harmony. A large factor in health or dis-ease patterns is the balance of earth, air, fire and water within our bodily systems.

Connecting the alter major with the throat chakra means that communication with our inner systems is enhanced, we can more easily hold our bodies in optimum health, and also be in touch with any developing imbalances before they become acute or chronic.

Nature Spirits

In different ways the alter major and throat chakras are connected to communication. When they work strongly together they enhance our communication with the natural world and the rhythms and life-force manifest in nature.

Comparatively little is known about the beings who are energetic guardians of the elemental and natural worlds. They are variously called devic beings, nature spirits, fairies, gnomes, elves, undines, nereids, salamanders and sprites. They have long been portrayed in stories and illustrations as part of our mythical consciousness. Devas are guardians of rivers, valleys, hillsides and trees. Fairies, elves, undines and nereids are energy beings with a sense of fun. They appear, to those who have 'the sight', in semi-human form when they want to attract attention and communicate. They are often bewildered when we do not see their flashes of light and colour or hear the tinkle of their laughter. Where there is energy, there *they* are. When all is well they work with the devas and direct their energies towards growth, fertility and abundance. When things are out of balance they are drawn to wherever the energy flow is strongest. Formed of basic energy, nature spirits on the lower levels of the hierarchy are primitively amoral and will pick up on, and accentuate, difficult as well as positive animation or interaction.

The hierarchy of nature spirits is on the same stream of consciousness as the angelic hierarchy – but there is a definite, more straightforward, evolutionary, two-way stream of consciousness amongst these beings than that within the human consciousness stream. Nature spirits and elementals are part of an energy streaming out from the Divine Source, but they also evolve *towards* the Source. The tiniest, amoral, 'dot' elementals will become fairies or undines and eventually part of one of the complex Devic forms. Devas become angels and evolve onwards through the angelic hierarchy. (For more on this, see my book *Working With Guides and Angels* in the Bibliography.)

Animals and Plants

When we are more aware of the subtle forces around us we also become aware of the role which animals and plants play in the universe. Scientifically, of course, with plants and trees we can understand the ways in which they balance the atmosphere and help to clean up reasonable levels of pollution. They are part of our food chain, as well as producing substances which are healing to our bodies. They communicate beauty and abundance to us and often inspire us to higher vision and understanding of universal patterns. When we respect, look after, and cooperate with plants we make a deeper commitment to incarnation and become more in touch with the earth and its natural rhythms and cycles.

We have a great karmic debt to animals and are collectively guilty of mistreating many of their species. We do not have to be vegetarians to be horrified at some of the conditions endured by factory-farmed animals or the plight of horses, dogs and cats who are starved or ill-treated. Only as species begin to die out do we seem to get any inkling of the value animals have in the balance of nature. Current campaigns to make us aware of the need to save particular animal species are reawakening an important awareness. If our alter major chakras had not 'gone to sleep' such crusades would not be necessary.

Gildas has spoken on several occasions of the importance of the sounds which animals make in supporting the subtle structure around us and in also helping to deal with, or prevent, pollution. The alter major/throat connection may not make us consciously hear all these subtle notes or appreciate the essential interaction of animal fragrances as part of planetary balance, but it will open us to an understanding that all factors within the natural world have a place in making the whole healthy. There are no accidents in the pattern of life. Human beings have made themselves dominant without always remembering that leadership should inspire and nourish, rather than crush and humiliate. Making the alter major/throat connection may lead us to some uncomfortable insights, but it is of the utmost energetic necessity if we are to live in harmony with all our relations – whatever their species.

ALTER MAJOR AND CROWN AS A CHAKRA PAIR

The main connection between alter major and crown is through their sharing of a subtle body. The crown is linked to the soul, ketheric or higher causal body, the alter major to the lower causal body which is a layer within the higher body.

The soul, ketheric or higher causal body holds the imprint of the intentions which we have made for this and other lifetimes. Whilst in incarnation, this layer can affect us through the subtle memories from other lives which cause us to react to positive or negative stimuli in ways which are not directly explicable in terms of our present life experience. Unexpectedly intense or so-called irrational fears, free-floating anxiety patterns, *déjà vu* experiences and exceptional giftedness are all examples of the interpenetration of the causal body into our lives.

The lower causal body of the alter major governs the rhythms chosen by our soul. Our birth will happen at a specific time and we will be preserved from death until our agreed lifespan has been reached. Awareness of, and communication with, this level of our beings, brings about a more immediate working out of the karmic laws of cause and effect, leaving less unfinished business to be balanced out in a future lifetime.

When alter major and crown are in balance, both causal layers are more integrated, and it is easier to achieve clarity about our life purpose.

ALTER MAJOR AND ROOT AS A CHAKRA PAIR

Connecting the alter major and root chakras increases our instinctual awareness. It puts us in touch with our positive animal nature, enabling us to sit more easily and naturally in our bodies and to trust them. When our living is out of tune with natural rhythms we can begin to fear the power of our bodies over us. The body has an instinctual wisdom and there is a deep sapience in dis-ease (see also Chapter 3). But when our bodies fail us, life can be complex indeed.

The connection of alter major to throat enables us to hear or apprehend the body's signallings, whereas the connection of alter major to root makes the signallings stronger and aids us in discerning, and surrendering to, our personal rhythms. When we are stressed it means that we have over-ridden those personal rhythms which are conducive to sustainable health. We do not all have the same constitution. Some of us thrive on stresses which others would find intolerable. When alter major and throat are connected we are more likely to live within our own capacities rather than striving to reach standards or norms of performance. We are also likely to be more tolerant of the patterns of others without wishing to compete or demand more.

In inner journeying it is sometimes suggested that a contact with an inner animal be made, since this signifies and symbolizes stronger connections with our natural instinctual nature. Knowing our inner 'body' power animal (see Glossary) can be helpful in the management of our bodies in today's stresses and unnatural rhythms. There is a guided visualization for this on page 236.

Case Study: Harmonizing with Nature

This case study is also written up in the alter major section of Working With Your Chakras *but I have no other which better fits the case for connecting the chakra pairs described in this chapter.*

I met James, a business executive, when I was working as a counsellor and healer in a residential natural health centre. He had become severely stressed and his blood pressure was dangerously high. He attended my daily relaxation classes and asked for some individual counselling sessions. His wife, Mary, was at the health centre too, giving James support and taking a much-needed break herself. She was desperately concerned and found her workaholic husband stressful to live with.

James found it difficult to relax. He was already wondering how to survive the remaining three weeks of the month for which he had booked. His 'normal' life consisted of a long commuter day. He took his lap-top computer and mobile phone with him wherever he went. Every journey was spent working. When he went abroad, he did not take Mary with him, nor did he allow himself time to see anything of the interesting places he visited. In the evenings or at weekends he was always to be found at his desk at home.

James had a lovely house on the edge of countryside, but never went for walks. He employed someone to help his wife with their large garden rather than get involved himself. He was reluctant to take holidays and, when persuaded to do so, the lap-top and sheafs of papers invariably went with him. On the few occasions that his wife could persuade him to go to the theatre or to socialize with friends, he was restless, irritable and abrupt.

Mary said that James only went outside on his way to the car, train or plane. She was sure that he was unaware of the seasons of the year – he wore lighter shirts and suits in summer only because she put them out for him.

When I told James that I was a healer as well as a counsellor he was surprisingly open to 'trying it out'. Perhaps he thought I could weave some magic which would allow him to go back to his old ways without making himself ill. I decided to work principally on his alter major chakra, encouraging it to open. The energy field at the back of his head felt tight, static and numb. I did some guided imagery with him, emphasizing natural scenes and the elements. Predictably, James found visualization difficult but playing quiet background music helped and he actually began to enjoy our sessions.

James was not the sort of person who would work directly with his chakras, but I taught him to massage the alter major positive polarity point gently with his fingertips. The health centre had extensive grounds, with cows and horses in adjoining fields and access to the sort of woods where the leaf-mould is thick and the scent of damp earth pervades. Mary encouraged James to walk in the woods with her and noticed that he was gradually becoming less restless and more able to converse with her in a relaxed way as they strolled through the greenery.

One day, Mary found James sitting on a bench, watching the cows chewing the cud. She sat near him and after a while he took her hand and said, 'All I really need to do is remember to watch the cows more often.' It was a true turning point. The combined treatments at the health centre were effective. James left with a much lower blood pressure reading, a determination to change his lifestyle, and a love of cows. Mary left with hope for her husband's future survival and for the quality of their life and marriage.

THE ARCHETYPES: PAN AND FLORA

Traditionally and mythologically, Pan is the king of the nature spirits and Flora his consort. They have a duality within them. Pan, in particular, sometimes appears as the eternal youth, playing his pipes, whilst flowers spring up to hear his tunes and mountains dance and sing – whilst at other times he prances around devilishly with cloven hooves, forked tail and enormous, erect phallus, creating the stuff of rape and nightmare.

Flora, though less changeable in her image, can be joyful, dancing and fertile, or negatively seductive, cruel and destructive.

When we are in tune with nature and our instincts, Pan and Flora bring us healing, harmony and celebration. They bless the earth and cause things to flourish. When we pollute the earth and deny our instincts, they rampage, wound and destroy. They are mirrors of ourselves and our relationship to natural worlds, rhythms and cycles. When we wound the earth and disrespect the natural kingdoms we eventually wound ourselves. If we see our instinctual drives, such as sexuality, as the shadow side of our natures then the shadow grows bigger than us and causes devastation.

Linking the chakra pairs discussed in this chapter helps us to keep the Pan/Flora energies in balance.

EXERCISES

Exercise 42
Linking the Throat and Alter Major Chakras

Sit or stand with your spine straight, your body symmetrically arranged and your feet uncrossed at knees or ankles, unless using a cross-legged or lotus posture.

- Begin with central column breathing (see page 17).
- Breathe in through your throat chakra petals and out through its stem (five to ten in/out breath sequences).
- Breathe in through the petals of your throat chakra to its centre. Hold your breath for a count of three, and then breathe up through your central column to the centre of your alter major chakra and out through its stem (five to ten in/out breath sequences).
- Breathe in through the stem of your alter major chakra and out through its petals (five to ten in/out breath sequences).
- Breathe in through the stem of your alter major chakra, holding your breath for a count of three in its centre. Breathe down into the centre of your throat chakra and out through its petals (five to ten in/out breath sequences).
- Finish with central column breathing, ending on the down-breath.

Exercise 43
Linking the Crown and Alter Major Chakras

Position yourself as for exercise 42, above.

- Begin with central column breathing.

- Breathe in through the stem of your alter major chakra and out through its petals (five to ten in/out breath sequences).
- Breathe in through the stem of your alter major chakra to its centre, hold your breath to a count of three. Breathe up through your central column and out through the petals of your crown chakra (five to ten in/out breath sequences).
- Breathe in through the petals of your crown chakra, down through your central column to the centre of your alter major chakra and out through its stem (five to ten in/out breath sequences).
- Finish with central column breathing, ending on the down-breath.

Exercise 44
Linking the Root and Alter Major Charkas

Position yourself as for Exercise 42 (see page 234).

- Begin with central column breathing (see page 17).
- Breathe up from the earth, through your root chakra, up your central column to the centre of your alter major chakra, and breathe out through the stem of your alter major chakra (five to ten in/out breath sequences).
- Breathe in through the stem of your alter major chakra and out through its petals (five to ten in/out breath sequences).
- Breathe in through the stem of your alter major chakra into its centre, holding your breath for a count of three. Breathe down through your central column, out through the petals of your root chakra and into the earth (five to ten in/out breath sequences).

- Finish with central column breathing, ending on the down-breath.

Exercise 45
Guided Visualization for Meeting Your Body Power Animal

According to Native American Indian tradition we each have a number of power or totem animals (see Glossary). One of them is particularly linked to our body and its health. This journey is specifically for meeting your body animal.

Making sure that you will be undisturbed, sit or lie in a comfortable balanced position with your body symmetrically arranged and your legs uncrossed at the knees or ankles, unless using a cross-legged or lotus posture. Have a blanket for warmth, and writing and drawing materials at hand.

- Be aware of the rhythm of your breathing . . . Gradually bring the rhythm into your heart centre and then travel on your heart breath into your inner landscape, finding yourself in your meadow . . .
- Activate all your inner senses so that you see the objects and colours . . . hear the sounds . . . smell the fragrances . . . touch the textures . . . and savour the tastes . . .
- From your meadow, you can see a wooded area of your landscape . . . A part of you knows where your body power animal dwells . . . Travel towards the wood and when you arrive there search for a damp part of the woods where there is a hole in the ground (perhaps by the roots of a tree), or for a damp, more rocky area where there are caves . . . Your body power animal lives either in the hole or in the cave to which you are instinctively led . . .
- Either call your animal to come out to meet you or go in to the hole or cave, taking a light with you if you wish.

Remember that, though your animal may be very wild or fierce in the outer world, in your inner world it is your friend and you can communicate with it . . . As you make each other's acquaintance ask your power animal to dance with you – a celebration of potential health, healing and well-being . . . *(Even if you are not well, or are unable to dance in the outer world, getting your power animal to dance in the inner world can aid the healing process.)*

Exercise 46
Considering Pan and Flora

- Take drawing and writing materials, make sure you will be undisturbed and, through creative writing, poetry or meditative drawing, connect to the positive side of Pan and/or Flora.
- As you write or draw, consider your relationship to celebration, jollity, sensuality and your knowledge of natural rhythms and cycles.
- Maybe plan to celebrate a solstice, equinox or one of the ancient festivals (see C.J. Cooper's *The Aquarian Dictionary of Festivals* in the Bibliography).

THE COLOURS

The colours for the alter major are brown, yellow ochre and olive green. They are denser tones than for other chakras but they should still be visualized as they would appear in stained glass with the light passing through it.

The brown is a deep brown ochre colour, with red tones in it. Positively, it helps to link us to the earth, to fertility, natural cycles and natural craftsmanship.

Negative tones of this colour can cause the onset of primitive fears and superstitions. They can engender primitive and forceful anger

Yellow ochre is the colour of deep mustard, often seen in lichens and tree fungi. Positively, it links us to the world of plants and herbal healing.

Negatively, this colour can be psychically toxic, making us out of touch with ourselves, our instincts and our self-healing mechanisms.

Olive green is the silvery green of the leaves of the olive tree rather than the colour of green olives. Positively, this colour brings us inner peace and strength and makes us confident in our bodies. It has no negative shades or powers.

The colours for the root chakra are red, brown and mauve.

The colours for the throat chakra are blue, silver and turquoise.

The colours for the crown chakra are violet, white and gold.

Use the colours as suggested in Exercise 8 (page 42) to develop, awaken and heal your chakras.

THE FRAGRANCES

For the alter major chakra the quietening fragrances are musk and cedarwood, and the stimulating ones are violet and rose-geranium.

Most of us need the stimulating fragrances for the alter major to help it become more open and active. These can be blended with one stimulating and one quietening fragrance from each of the other pairs to stimulate the pair connections. James's alter major chakra was quite tightly closed. His masseur at the health clinic added a mixture of lavender and amber oils to the usual massage oil.

A few people are so attuned to the elements and natural earth rhythms that they seem almost like sprites in appearance and movement or in a 'butterfly' attitude to life. In these cases the alter major chakra may be disproportionately active and the quietening fragrances should be used.

For the root chakra the quietening fragrances are cedarwood and patchouli, and the stimulating ones are musk, lavender and hyacinth. For the throat chakra the quietening fragrances are lavender and hyacinth, and the stimulating ones are patchouli and white musk. For the crown chakra the quietening fragrances are rosemary and bergamot, and the stimulating ones are violet and amber.

THE CRYSTALS

Refer to page 44 and the Glossary for general guidance on using crystals. The crystals which will best help the issues considered in this chapter are:

Fossils (polished or natural) To help us connect to morphic resonance and the wisdom stored in the collective unconscious. They promote our natural relationship with other species.

Carnelian To encourage contact with nature spirits, aid our memory of other lifetimes and help us to dream 'great dreams' (sleep dreams which have a wider relevance than the merely personal).

Turquoise To help our communication with all that is natural and also aid the connection with our body animals.

PRAYERS OR AFFIRMATIONS

The alter major chakra prayer or affirmation is:

Through engagement with our Devic Nature may we move from duality and split, to oneness and unity.

The root chakra prayer or affirmation is:

Through incarnation may spirit be brought into matter. Through rootedness may life force be recharged and exchanged. We acknowledge wholeness and seek to gain and to reflect acceptance.

The throat chakra prayer or affirmation is:

Help us to develop responsibility. May universal truth impregnate causal action so that the voice of humanity may find true harmony with the voice of the earth.

The crown chakra prayer or affirmation is:

Through surrender and release let the incoming will be truly the will of God working within us and through us, leading us increasingly to knowledge of mystical union and mystical marriage.

For suggestions on using prayers or affirmations see page 45.

Chapter 12

New Dimensions:
Death and Rebirth

Key Issues: Death and Rebirth, Chaos, New Opportunities, the
Millenium, the Birth of New Archetypes
Chakra System: The New Chakras, the Base, the Hara, the
Unconditional Love Centre, the Third Eye
The Archetypes: Unconditional Love, the Fool

This chapter will help you:
- learn about the more recently discovered chakras
- Understand the place of chaos in the scheme of things
- learn about possibilities for the new millennium, new opportunities and the birth of new archetypes

---

AREAS OF INFLUENCE

The Base Chakra
Location Petals over the pubic bone, stem at the coccyx
Key Words Retribution, Redemption, Choice, Transition,
Peace, The World

Developmental Age Conception to Birth
Colours Deep Rose Red, Ruby, Purple
Element Earth
Body Causal
Quietening Fragrances Heather, Rosewood
Stimulating Fragrances Lemon Verbena, Thyme
Crystals and Gemstones Rhodocrosite, Moonstone, Rose Quartz. Rose Opal, Rubilite

Prayer or Affirmation

We acknowledge the interaction of our soul choice for retribution with our psychological environment. We seek to understand and surrender to the transition form retribution to redemption.

The Hara Chakra

Location In the auric field between the sacral and solar plexus chakras
Key Words Vitality, Power, Healing, Regeneration, Balance, God
Colours Apricot, Silver, Platinum
Element Granite
Quietening Fragrances Hibiscus, Apricot
Stimulating Fragrances Frankincense, Lily of the Valley
Crystals and Gemstones Honey Calcite, Sunstone, Iron Pyrites' Sun, Stibnite, Wulfenite

Prayer or Affirmation

We acknowledge and connect with the universal vital lifeforce. We accept our potential for health and regeneration, knowing that release from disease will bring collective self-actualization.

The Unconditional Love Centre

Location Within and extending the usual heart chakra
Key Words Wisdom, Unconditional Love, Self-Realization, Discrimination, Integrity
Colours Rose, Amethyst, Pearlized Mauve
Element Sea Water
Quietening Fragrances Orchid, Camomile
Stimulating Fragrances Geranium, Basil
Crystals and Gemstones Amethyst, Sugilite (also called Luvulite), Lepidolite, Dolomite, Alexandrite

Prayer or Affirmation

We open ourselves to the blessing of unconditional love. We accept that we are unconditionally loved. We ask that we may practise unconditional love without loss of integrity or wise discrimination. Help us to emerge from complacency.

The Third Eye Chakra

Location A vortex chakra, in the auric field, out from and slightly above the brow chakra
Key Word Beauty, Justice, Guardianship, Transformation
Colours Silvery Blue, Indigo, Magenta
Element Spiritual Fire
Quietening Fragrances Carnation, Poppy
Stimulating Fragrances Jasmine, Sage
Crystals and Gemstones Optical Calcite, Ellelstials, Herkimer Diamond, Fluorite Double Pyramids

Prayer or Affirmation

We commit ourselves to vision. In this commitment we acknowledge that the vision of the past empowers the vision of the present and that the vision of the present enables the vision of the future. In service of that vision we ask the gifts of beauty and justice so that the structures of our security may be flexible and renewable. In making gold from the dross of life and experience, may we do so without despising the dross itself.

THE NEW CHAKRAS

For some years Gildas and other channelled sources have suggested that the major chakra system needs to expand to twelve, rather than having seven or eight chakras within its team. Of course, 'new' chakras, like 'new' planets, have long been there but have remained undiscovered or unawakened. Now, as we are about to enter a new millennium, it is especially important to awaken the chakra resources which will help us find the spiritual strength to sustain ourselves through change, crisis and possibly chaos.

The new chakras do not form pairs or triads in quite the same way as those within the original major team. They form a system of their own, and it is this we need to consider and work with in our times. There are no case studies for the new chakras yet, since they are, comparatively, so newly awakening. Each one of us who seeks a spiritual perspective as we stand on the brink of quantum change is a potential case study for the new chakras.

My previous book *Working With Your Chakras* examined each of the new chakras in as much detail as possible. In this book, I want, rather, to look at the ways in which they support each other in their 'team within a team'.

Each new chakra gives us certain resources for the times in which we live. As we develop their qualities, and the energies from these chakras flow into our present energy bodies, so our very substance will change.

Whichever chakras exist for us as a collective, or as individuals, also exist within the substance of the planet on which we live. As the new earth chakras awaken, so the substance and vibrational rate of matter will change and some of our present theories of physical law and science will become redundant.

Chaos

To some of us, such new possibilities will seem exciting. To others, such predictions may bring fear and insecurity. If apparently proven laws and even our own bodies are going to change, how shall we survive the chaos which will ensue? Traditionally we fear chaos as we fear evil but, as we awaken to the potential of a New Age, we need to see it as a natural law. When, recently and excitingly, the patterns of chaos were caught on film, a new perspective on chaos had to be embraced. Its swirls and movements can be extremely beautiful; far from being completely disorganized, chaos already holds the new order which it is actively seeking, within its intricate patternings.

The new chakra energies will sustain us and give us the tools and courage to enter the chaos, find its beauty, acknowledge it as one of the wonders of Divine manifestation and emerge, ourselves, renewed and freed from the debris of the old order, into the new potential.

Death and Rebirth

All too often, when we think of death, we think of loss. We are not yet used to the realization that within all death lies potential rebirth. We too rarely speak of death and rebirth in the same breath. Yet the new chakras teach us more than ever that allowing death also enables birth. Clinging to old structures simply because we are afraid to take risks produces debris and detritus which blocks the birth channels.

New Opportunities

When we see a horizon we tend to think that it marks the end of something – it can become a boundary for us. As we look towards the symbolic horizon of the old order, we may fear that beyond it can lie only darkness and destruction. Yet, in real life, horizons move. As we journey, the horizon is constantly changing as our experience of the landscape grows greater. As we approach the place of quantum change, we must have faith that the horizons are not ultimate boundaries, but a measure of how far we have come and a sign that there is always further to go.

Gildas says that we must be as courageous as the first Elizabethan explorers who set out to prove that the world was not flat. With far fewer resources than we have now, they bravely went over the horizon, did not fall over the edge, and returned with new knowledge to the place from which they had set out, knowing that place as they had never known it before, because they were now seeing it in the context of something more than they had ever been able to imagine.

THE BIRTH OF NEW ARCHETYPES

We have seen, throughout this book, that archetypes are related to Divine Principles. As we grow able to 'discover' new chakras, new planets, new concepts, new horizons, so can we expect to discover new Divine Principles and bring them into practice. If it is time for the archetypes of guru and devotee to die (see page 194), then it is time for the archetype of unconditional love to come to full fruition. When this happens we shall be fully able to support each other as the quantum leap is made, since old hierarchies based on greed, jealousy and false power will drop away.

Perhaps another archetype, which is being born, is the positive aspect of chaos. Previously we have related only to the shadow side of this, because, by its very nature, it is so difficult to differentiate.

The Archetype of Unconditional Love

This archetype is newly awakening. We have to learn to see it not only as something we aspire to practise, but as something which encompasses each one of us. It can be surprisingly challenging and demanding to know oneself unconditionally loved. Many of us will be able to identify an inner part which would rather be punished, shaped and told what to do by a higher authority. Unconditional love for all demands that we take self-responsibility and live only from the highest within us. Scarily, this means making our own decisions and trusting in an inherent integrity to help us to know what that may be, at each step of the way.

The unconditional love centre, as a new chakra, is the energy point where we learn to receive and incorporate the energy of unconditional love. The emphasis must be on learning to receive this quality with grace. If we see unconditional love as something we must give, before we are able to receive it, then we shall be in danger of patronizing and subtly judging each other.

The Archetype of the Fool

The fool is not a new archetype, yet is coming into a new potency. When we view the fool we must question and re-question all our values and assumptions, for the fool is the one who jumps empty-handed into the abyss – and always lands on his feet. He makes us constantly question, what is innocence, what is magic and what is irresponsibility? If debated or meditated upon deeply, these are not comfortable questions to have to answer, but the coming time is going to make each one of us wish the archetype of the fool to be our true ally.

THE DIMENSIONS GIVEN BY THE NEW CHAKRAS

The Dimension Given by the Base Chakra

As the new age dawns, so karma will change. The base chakra energies, when active within our beings, enable us to leave old, retributive, 'eye for an eye and tooth for a tooth' karmic patterns behind. We shall not, in the future, be bound to the wheel of rebirth in the same way.

We choose our own karmic tasks for a lifetime, when, in the

between-life state we have reviewed the life we have just lived. We are our own taskmasters. We often choose to receive that which we (in another personality bead from the soul stem) have meted out to others. Such a choice is made when we are still attached to the old order and the old treadmill of rebirth.

Alongside unconditional love, goes self-forgiveness and a recognition that each one of us has been, and continues, on a journey of experience. All the experience which we have had, or caused, has been of benefit to the total journey of humanity; therefore we do not need to perpetuate patterns by reaping what we have sown. It is often the nature of the present karmic pattern that we cannot reap exactly what we have sown unless someone else is put in the position of sowing the same pattern so that we can reap it. This becomes a vicious pattern, a weary treadmill indeed, rather than a spiral of transcendence. We need to bring new seed into incarnation with us, learn the non-attachment to our deeds and misdeeds which is transcendence, and so allow the birth of the Divine Principle of unconditional love to live us, as we live *it*.

The Dimension Given by the Hara Chakra

The hara chakra offers us the amazing potential of regeneration. When we fully comprehend this, and allow it to course through our physical and spiritual veins, we shall have perfect choice over life and death, since our bodies will remain in optimum condition for the whole of our incarnate lifespan. We shall not age and die, but will have, instead, the responsibility of choosing when we judge our life task or service on earth to be finished or entering a new phase. We shall then make a conscious transition to the next phase of learning, rather in the same way as our guides, in their dimension, do now.

The Dimension Given by the Third Eye

The brow chakra is often confused with the third eye. Though the brow gives us spiritual vision and is necessary to the functioning of the third eye, they are not one and the same energy centre. The third eye is a vortex in the auric energy field, with energetic support links to and from other chakras.

Having an open third eye does not mean, as some people mistakenly assume, that we have instant access to past lives, future events, astral travel, shifts in states of consciousness, gifts of diagnosis and healing of disease, the ability to see auras, nature spirits and angels, and commune easily with guides. Most of these faculties are psychic in origin, rather than spiritual. A spiritual dimension can only truly be added when we cease to be diverted by the glamour of phenomena (see also page 164).

Having an open third eye simply means being able to see life from a clear spiritual perspective; maintaining hope, faith and balance in a confusing and changing world; having a concept of oneself as a responsible spiritual guardian – and having the will to develop the strength for such a task; perceiving the inner quality of others without judgment – and never losing faith in the perfection and beneficence of the divine plan in which each one of us is included. When all these qualities have been developed and, paradoxically, phenomena have no attraction for their own sake – then the phenomena will manifest anyway.

THE NEW MILLENNIUM

The changes of which our guides speak are certainly predicted to come during the first phase of the new millennium. I suspect that the dawn of the millennium itself will not be an immediate magic threshold – yet in its birth lies its potential. As the old millennium dies, we have an enormous opportunity to leave old patterns behind and make new choices. The potential for a golden age for humanity will certainly lie in the new millennium's blueprint. Collectively, we shall soon be midwives and parents to an infant prodigy. What is there, in nature, needs to be brought out and supported by nurture. When we, as individuals, work with our new chakras we prepare ourselves for this exciting but momentous task.

WORKING WITH THE NEW CHAKRAS

With each of the new chakras, the work, as yet, remains very simple. These chakras need to be strengthened and awakened. Therefore they need to have their colours breathed into them; their crystals used (by selecting a crystal and holding it over the chakra area for five or ten minutes); their fragrances diffused into our environment and absorbed into our energy systems; and their prayers or affirmations repeated and meditated upon.

The quietening and stimulating fragrances for each of the chakras should be mixed together for the new chakras – as such, they will form a balancing or awakening fragrance for the chakra. Experiment with finding a balance of a few drops of each, which you find pleasant and harmonizing.

Working with the Base Chakra

No specific exercise is given here for the base chakra; simply use its colours, crystals, fragrances and affirmation as suggested above. Doing so will help the base chakra become an active member of your chakra team.

The Base Chakra Colours

The colours for the base chakra are deep rose red, ruby and purple.

Deep rose red is often seen in our rose gardens. Positively, it warms and welcomes.

Negatively, it can speak of wounding and over-vulnerability.

Ruby is the colour of the gemstone of the same name and

of deep red wine. Positively, it is a colour which leads us to seek and respect our inner depths.

Negatively, it can be a suffocating colour, absorbing everything and cutting us off from positive resonances.

Purple is bright, but less brilliant than the violet of the crown chakra. Positively, it enhances the quality of self-worth.

Negatively, it overpowers and disempowers.

As you breathe the colours into your base chakra, remember to visualize them as stained glass appears when sunlight passes through it.

The Crystals for the Base Chakra

Refer to page 44 and the Glossary for general guidance on using crystals. The crystals which will best help the issues considered in this chapter are:

Rhodocrosite This stone has a gentle energy. It promotes our ability to love the earth and to recognize the interaction of spirit with matter.

Moonstones For the base chakra, moonstones should be slightly pink in tone. They help us to make transitions and to move from retributive to redemptive karma.

Rose Quartz A comforting crystal. At the base chakra it helps to keep connections with our guardian angel alive.

Rose Opal To facilitate birth; useful for mothers during labour, but also aids the birth of ideas and new phases of life or rites of passage.

Rubilite To assist our memory of the spiritual worlds and planes. It encourages us to incorporate beauty and sacred dimensions into the things we create and the buildings we build.

Working with the Vortex Chakras

The hara and the third eye chakras have a different structure from the chakras of the usual system. They are vortices, in the energy field, supported by important energy links to other major and minor chakra points. To build these structures, see Exercise 47 on page 253 and Exercise 48 on page 255.

The Hara Chakra Colours

The hara chakra colours are apricot, silver and platinum. Apricot is the colour of ripe apricots, soft and warm in tone. Positively, it enhances the body's ability to heal itself and brings a sense of well-being. It has no negative aspects or tones.

Silver is the soft silver glow of the precious metal. It give flexibility with strength. At the hara there are no negative qualities to silver.

Platinum, though similar to silver, is rather more blue in tone. Symbolically, it means stamina and endurance.

The Crystals for the Hara Chakra

Refer to page 44 and the Glossary for general guidance on using crystals. The crystals which will best help the issues considered in this chapter are:

Honey Calcite To encourage balance; helps to strengthen the energy supports which the hara needs for optimal functioning.

Sun Stone This crystal facilitates receptivity to energy from the universal source. It stimulates self-healing abilities.

Iron Pyrites Suns These are comparatively rare forms of the pyrites family and are flat gold disks with shining rays coming from a central point. They facilitate resistance to stress.

Stibnite A useful crystal for healers, stibnite has a metallic, striated appearance. It enables a steady flow of energy to others and helps in cultivating a calm, refreshing presence.

Wulfenite This is associated with the hara because of its apricot colouring. It strengthens the auric field. It helps those in positions of authority to temper power with compassion.

Exercise 47
Building the Energetic Structure for the Hara Chakra Vortex

For this exercise it is important to be sitting in an upright position, with your back supported if necessary. Unless using a cross-legged or lotus posture, do not cross your legs at the knees or ankles.

- Begin with central column breathing (see page 17).
- Focus your attention into your sacral chakra and concentrate on letting its petals open flexibly.
- Move your awareness up, through your central column to your solar plexus centre. Let these petals open.
- Move your attention slightly upwards and to the left and locate an energy centre over your spleen.
- Move your attention over to the right of your body and feel the energy centre over your liver.
- Imagine spiralling strands of golden energy streaming from each of these centres into your auric field, and meeting at a point in front of and above your sacral chakra but below your solar plexus. Concentrate until you can feel this structure getting clear and strong. Working for a few minutes each day will be more successful eventually than trying too hard at any single session.
- When your structure is well established, you will naturally become aware of the hara vortex itself, opening, spinning and returning vitality through the spiralling lines of connection to the vital organs of your body. You do not need to close the hara centre down, it will regulate itself according to your needs.

Working with the Third Eye Chakra

The Colours for the Third Eye Chakra

The colours for the third eye chakra are silvery blue, indigo and magenta. Silvery blue has a metallic quality and is the colour seen in peacock stone (bornite or chalcopyrites).

Positively, silvery blue enhances vision.

Negatively, it is a cold colour which can breed harsh, cold detachment.

Indigo is as for the brow chakra on page 201.

Magenta is a reddish violet. It is thought to have a higher vibration than violet, which is usually seen as the highest vibrational colour in the spectrum. It is probably, therefore, the first colour in a new octave of the spectrum, to reveal itself to us.

Positively, magenta lifts the spirit. It has no negative qualities, though may be over-stimulating for some people.

The Crystals for the Third Eye Chakra

Refer to page 44 and the Glossary for general guidance on using crystals. The crystals which will best help the issues considered in this chapter are:

Optical Calcite A clear version of calcite, with a rhomboid form, this crystal breaks light into the spectrum of colour and is therefore full of rainbows. True to its name, it aids clear sight and vision of a spiritual nature.

Ellestials These are among the more recent crystal discoveries. They have a similar appearance to smoky quartz but their form is square and flat. They form close clusters and often have water trapped within them. They are crystals which inspire and encourage us to reach our highest potential.

Herkimer Diamond This is a member of the quartz family. They are diamond-shaped crystals, usually quite small and clear, as though having been polished and faceted. They are only mined in Herkimer County, New York State, and grow in liquid solution. They enhance all spiritual qualities, give vitality and encourage joy.

Fluorite Double Pyramids Also diamond-shaped, these crystals aid the development of spiritual awareness and help to transform spiritual ideas into material reality. They come in different shades, mainly white, purple, mauve and green. The white or purple are most suitable for the third eye.

Exercise 48
Building the Subtle Structure for the Third Eye

Position yourself as for Exercise 47, page 253.

- Begin with central column breathing (see page 17).
- Imagine your auric energy field, stretching out about 4–6 inches from your physical body. Sense the area where your brow chakra petals emerge into this field.
- Focus your attention a little above and beyond the petals of your brow chakra and seek an intense energy spot in your auric field, or a moving vortex of spiralling energy.
- Visualize the colours silvery blue, indigo and magenta around this area.
- Visualize a line of energy going from this energy spot or vortex into your brow chakra and through, to connect with your pineal gland (see page 186). Breathe along this line (two to three in/out breaths).
- Imagine another line of energy running from the third eye position, up to your crown chakra. Breathe along this line (two to three in/out breaths).
- Visualize a line of energy going from the third eye, through

the petals of your alter major chakra, and into its stem. Breathe along this line (two to three in/out breaths).

- Visualize a line of energy going from your third eye vortex into your throat chakra. Breathe along this line (two to three in/out breaths).
- Return your attention to your third eye point and sense it clearing and strengthening.
- Feel your feet in contact with the ground and visualize a cloak of light with a hood right around you.
- You do not need to close down the third eye vortex – it will regulate itself.

Working with the Unconditional Love Centre

This chakra, too, has a new form, since it is a chakra within a chakra. The basic meditation for opening and contacting the unconditional love centre is given as Exercise 49 on page 257.

The Colours for the Unconditional Love Centre

The colours for the unconditional love centre are rose, amethyst and pearlized mauve. Rose is a tender, but full-bodied pink. Positively, it brings a sense of security and acceptance.

Negatively, it can smother.

Amethyst at the unconditional love centre is the colour seen in paler-toned or 'lavender' amethyst crystals. This colour encourages qualities of fine discernment. It has no negative qualities or tones.

Pearlized mauve is also light-toned, with a pearlized sheen. It is the colour given out by lepidolite crystals. It is a protective colour and also encourages high aspiration. It has no negative tones or qualities.

The Crystals for the Unconditional Love Centre

Refer to page 44 and the Glossary for general guidance on using crystals. The crystals which will best help the issues considered in this chapter are:

Amethyst When chosen for the unconditional love centre, this crystal should be pale or slightly greyish. It helps the centre to awaken, whilst also strengthening and protecting it.

Sugilite/Luvulite Comparatively rare; facilitates self-acceptance and encourages the development of feelings of unconditional love for self and others.

Lepidolite A form of mica which aids self-forgiveness and release, which are often necessary before unconditional love can develop.

Dolomite To strengthen the unconditional love centre and encourage the growth of integrity.

Alexandrite To help in the cultivation of wise discrimination.

Exercise 49
Guided Visualization for the Unconditional Love Centre

Sit or lie down in a comfortable position with your body symmetrically arranged and your legs uncrossed at the knees or ankles unless you are using a cross-legged or lotus posture.

- Be in touch with the rhythm of your breathing . . . Gradually let this rhythm help you to bring the focus of your attention into your heart chakra . . . Visualize each petal of the chakra opening rhythmically with each in-breath and out-breath . . .
- Enter your own inner space and find yourself looking into a large, delicately scented pink rose . . . Notice the texture of the petals . . . Each one is tipped with a delicate touch of green . . . The centre of the rose is pure gold . . .

- The rose becomes large enough for you to enter it . . . The gold in its centre becomes a golden gateway through which you can pass . . . into a garden beyond . . . You find yourself in a rose garden, full of mauve and pink roses . . . It is formally laid out, with grassed alleyways along which to walk and wooden seats under rose arbours . . . Spend little time exploring this fragrant place and perhaps sit for a while in one of its arbours . . .

- Now you see a path which you had not noticed before and you decide to follow it . . . You leave the formal part of the garden and come to some rocks which shine with a pearly mauve light . . . Ahead of you there is a rocky archway with an angel-like figure standing there . . . As you come near the archway and the light being you know that you are welcome and that this guardian is not here to keep you out, but to welcome you in and protect you as you enter a sacred space . . .

- You can now see an amethyst crystal temple . . . As you come near, the door opens and you go inside . . . Amethyst crystals are all around you and the atmosphere is warm and welcoming . . . You feel totally vulnerable and yet totally safe . . . You know that you are fully accepted, fully seen and unconditionally loved . . . Bask in this knowledge and feeling for a while . . .

- When you are ready, retrace your steps . . . out of the crystal temple, past the guardian at the archway, back through the formal rose garden to its golden gateway . . . go through the gateway . . . and become aware again of your own breath in your heart chakra . . . Let the petals of this centre fold in, and put a star or cross of light in a circle of light over it as a blessing . . . Feel the contact of your feet with the ground and gradually ease back into your normal environment . . .

THE LAST WORD

It seems appropriate to end the book on this note – the opening of the unconditional love centre in preparation for the millennium which will bring us the changes long predicted (if not immediately, then perhaps in the foreseeable future and in the present lifetimes of many of us). Working with chakra pairs and triads and the new chakras brings energy and development not only for each of us personally, but also for the whole of humanity and the earth itself.

The Gildas Prayer

Let light from the Source shine into the darknesses of earth and bring healing

Let love from the Source shine into our hearts and bring peace and harmony

Let the force of Light, tempered with love, enter into our minds, that the things of our own creation may more truly reflect the Divine

Let light and love, peace and strength, healing and harmony bring at last that union with the Source which passes all understanding

Let understanding, born of peace and harmony, light and love, encompass the earth, now and forever. Amen.

Glossary

Alchemy This is a tradition which originated in Persia. In Europe, in the Middle Ages, alchemists were seen as being engaged on research which would enable lead (base metal) to be transformed into gold. Undoubtedly some, usually called 'puffers and blowers', undertook such research. However, true spiritual alchemy uses the imagery of base metal being transformed into gold as a basis for complex esoteric teaching about the journey and evolution of the soul.

Crystals Natural crystals, such as clear quartz, amethyst, rose quartz and aventurine, are reminders to us of the spirit which resides in matter. Crystals, used as an aid to spiritual work and healing, enhance and amplify. Crystals also have active healing energies within them. These are released when we declare our healing intention, and then use the crystal to help us focus on that intention, that area of the body or our chakras.

Crystals are readily available from many different shops, suppliers or market stalls. Use the crystal sections in each chapter to help you to decide which varieties of stones you would like to acquire. When you have found a source, rely on your intuition to tell you which, of a particular variety, is the right crystal for you.

Spend some time getting to know your crystal. Look at it carefully, handle it, admire it. When you are ready to prepare it for serious work, wait until three days before the full moon when you should put it into water containing a little sea salt. Do not do this with crystals mounted as jewellery, with synthetic cystals, or with those which feel soft or flaky – such as some pieces of lepidolite. These can be frequently rinsed in running water during this period or placed on a large, previously cleansed, amethyst cluster.

On the night of the full moon, dry your crystal on silk or soft cotton and put it in the garden or on the windowsill. Even if the full moon is behind cloud, your crystal will absorb what it needs. After this, it should be 'charged' by twelve hours of sunlight. (Behind glass is fine, but the light should shine as directly as possible onto the crystals, which should be turned regularly.) This charging can be done intermittently until twelve hours' worth of sun has been absorbed.

In a simple ceremony dedicate each of your crystals to its purpose. Light a candle, hold the stone for a while in your cupped hands, and then ask it to help in your development or healing.

(For fuller information see Soozi Holbeche's *The Power of Gems and Crystals* in the Bibliography.)

Higher Self Our higher self is, in essence, the part of our consciousness or soul which does not incarnate. The higher self has an overview of all our lifetimes and decides our task and purpose in each incarnation.

Inner Journeying Guided journeys for self-exploration require, but also enable, a slightly altered state of consciousness in which the focus of our attention may be inwardly directed. They help us to become progressively more familiar with 'what is inside' – or what is often termed the 'inner landscape'.

Through guided journeying, not only is information from within brought to the surface, but self-healing and enhancement of spiritual consciousness can become more personally directed or controlled. There is a time and tide, a rhythm or cycle in all things, but when the tide is right we need to use it as skilled surfers, rather than as flotsam and jetsam to be taken only where the wave wills. Each stage of an inner journey or series of journeys leads you a little more deeply into yourself in order to 'clear' psychological material and reveal the next steps on your spiritual path.

In the inner journeys of this book 'safety factors' are built into the method of journeying. Relaxing and aligning your physical body helps to balance your chakras and subtle energies. Though it may sometimes seem repetitive, beginning in the meadow means that there is a safe place at the edge of normal waking consciousness and the inner worlds. Before you do any serious journeying, you connect with the meadow and activate your inner senses. Before you return to the outer world you pass through the meadow, thus signalling to yourself that you are about to move from one area of your consciousness to another. If at any time you feel uncomfortable with anything in your inner world, then the meadow is there as the safe area of transition. There you can peacefully consider the inner happenings or rest awhile before you ease over into the demands of your outer world.

In the induction to each inner journey, irrespective of which chakra pair or triad it may be aimed at, you are guided to open up your heart centre or chakra. The heart energy is a particularly safe and wise energy on which to travel. Activating it ensures that your experiences will be gentle and that you will only unveil those secrets of your psyche which you are able to deal with at any given time.

Do not be tempted to use inner journeys for 'digging' into your past or memory. Accept what comes. If you are enthusiastic about psychological and spiritual unfolding, it is tempting to test the boundaries and to force blocked memories to the surface. But the psyche is very wise and reveals its depths only in an environment of trust. When you remember something during an inner journey, even if it seems very familiar or mundane, your psyche will have a reason for giving you that memory at that time. If you respect this and work with what is given, then gradually and gently the deeper revelations will also emerge. Trauma and drama are not measurements of depth or speed of growth.

Symbols used in the induction to journeys, such as a talisman or amulet, an inner wise being or a power animal, help to evoke the power, strength or wisdom in your psyche. They help you to journey wisely and to be centred as you do so. If you are at a crossroads or have any kind of choice to make during a journey, these aspects of yourself will help you find the right direction and make the right choice.

The Amulet This is similar to a talisman and has a related function. You can have an amulet as well as, or instead of, a talisman. Whilst a talisman is something that has *become* special or meaningful to you, an amulet may have been charged or blessed in some way and is usually given to you by someone special or to mark a special moment. Like the talisman, the amulet may exist in the outer world as well as the inner. It is most likely to be a piece of jewellery, a precious stone or crystal, a beautiful bottle or casket, a jewelled knife, a sword or chalice.

The talisman or amulet may remain constant and unchanging in your journeys or there may be special gifts for particular journeys. Most people who journey in the inner worlds end up with quite a collection of inner treasures!

The Power Animal The concept of the power animal has its roots in shamanistic lore. Animals can help us in our inner worlds. They protect us, guide us, mirror lessons for us, and help us to stay in contact with our natural sense of what is right, wholesome and safe. With their aid we can see in the dark, swim under water whilst still breathing, fly and glide on air currents, walk through the fire and survive the swamp or the pit. The strong yet gentle power animals of our inner worlds may be very wild or fierce in the outer. When we cross the threshold to inner experience they become our friends, they may speak to us and become our guides and protectors.

It is possible to meet animals in our inner worlds who are not friendly because they symbolize some inner conflict or imbalance, but the true power animal can always be trusted, will come when we call, track us when we stray, energize us when we are fatigued, and help to heal us when we are ill. They are recognized by the light in their eyes and their joy at being found by us, or invited into the journey.

The Talisman This may be a reflection of something which also comforts you in the outer world. For some it is their childhood teddy bear or rocking horse, conveniently miniaturized or even animated for easier travel. For others the talisman may be more archetypal or classical, like a guiding star, a staff or lantern. It does not matter what form it takes, but it must have the ability to give you a feeling of safety and comfort whenever you touch it.

The Inner Wise Presence In our good moments, when we make clear decisions or give wise, non-judgmental advice to a friend, we know that we have access to a place of wisdom within. It has little to do with personal experience and is related to a knowledge of inner potential and the potential of humankind. In inner journeys this source of wisdom becomes personified. It may be a mythological being or animal, or it may simply be an atmosphere of sacredness and love. By learning in the inner worlds that we can call this being or presence to us at will, we can be led to deeper layers of self-understanding as well as being empowered to use its strength more often and more consciously in outer life.

Karma This is the spiritual law of cause and effect (which defies 'nutshell definition'). 'As you sow, so shall you reap', gives a basic but over-simplified idea. Belief in karma goes alongside belief in reincarnation and personal, progressive evolution. The tendency is to see karma as something troublesome or heavy which needs to be overcome during a specific lifetime – but giftedness or innate wisdom are positive karmic attributes.

Psyche Analytic and transpersonal psychologies have shown how complex the human personality is. The psyche refers to the total being, with all its drives, needs, conflicts, dis-ease, health, gifts and potential.

Shadow The part of the 'I' which we do not admit into full consciousness. That which is unconscious, undefined, formless, dark, shadowy and without concept; the unknown.

Tarot An ancient form of cards which can be 'read' for the purposes of divination. The seventy-two cards form a major and a minor arcana. The major arcana consists of twenty-two archetypes covering all aspects of human experience. The minor arcana has four suits, differently named in different sets of cards, but mostly representative of mind, body, emotions and spirit. The twenty-two archetypes of the major arcana are: the Fool, the Magician, the High Priestess, the Empress, the Emperor, the Hierophant, the Lovers, the Chariot, Strength, the Hermit, the Wheel of Fortune, Justice, the Hanged Man, Death, Temperance, the Devil, the Tower, the Star, the Moon, the Sun, Judgment, the World.

Tibetan Singing Bowls These beaten brass bowls traditionally come from Tibet, where making them is an art form. When vibrated or struck, the bowls give out clear sounds, accompanied by overtones and undertones, which 'sing' on or continue resonating for an unusual length of time. The sounds are healing and often helpful in chakra work.

Transpersonal Therapy and Counselling This addresses the spiritual needs and aspirations of human beings as well as the behavioural. It concentrates on the importance of finding a meaning in life and of being creative and fulfilled in living, relating and making choices.

Yin and Yang These are Chinese words for the basic but opposite aspects of creation. Yin is receptive, feminine and dark. Yang is active, masculine and light. In the traditional yin/yang symbol one black and one white fish-like shape nestle together to form a perfect circle. The eye of the black shape is white and the eye of the white shape is black, showing that the seed of each is contained in the other.

Bibliography

Books by Ruth White
A Message of Love, London: Piatkus Books, 1989.
The River of Life, York Beach, ME: Samuel Weiser, 1997.
A Question of Guidance, Saffron Walden, England: C. W. Daniel, 1989.
Working with Your Chakras, York Beach, ME: Samuel Weiser, 1995.
Working with Your Guides and Angels, York Beach, ME: Samuel Weiser, 1997.

By Ruth White with Mary Swainson
Gildas Communicates, Saffron Walden, England: C. W. Daniel, 1971.
The Healing Spectrum, Saffron Walden, England: C. W. Daniel, 1979.
Seven Inner Journeys, Saffron Walden, England: C. W. Daniel, 1975.

Recommended Reading
Bailey, Alice. *Discipleship in the New Age,* London: The Lucis Press, 1966.
Cooper, C. J. *The Aquarian Dictionary of Festivals,* London: Aquarian Press, 1990.
———. *An Illustrated Encyclopaedia of Symbols,* London: Thames and Hudson, n. d.
Ferrucci, Pierro (disciple of Assagioli). *What We May Be,* London: Thorsons, 1989.
Heider, John. *The Tao of Leadership,* Atlanta, GA: Humanics, 1985.
Jung, C. G. *Man and His Symbols,* New York: Dell, 1968.
Krystall, Phyllis. *Cutting the Ties that Bind,* York Beach, ME: Samuel Weiser, 1993.
Holbeche, Soozie. *The Power of Gems and Crystals,* London: Piatkus Books, 1989.
Raphaell, Katharina. *Crystal Enlightenment,* Santa Fe, NM: Aurora Press, 1985.
———. *Crystal Healing,* Santa Fe, NM: Aurora Press, 1987.

Index